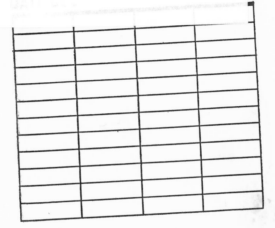

Laurence Sterne's
Tristram Shandy

Edited and with an introduction by

Harold Bloom
Sterling Professor of the Humanities
Yale University

Chelsea House Publishers ◊ *1987*

NEW YORK ◊ NEW HAVEN ◊ PHILADELPHIA

© 1987 by Chelsea House Publishers, a division
of Chelsea House Educational Communications, Inc.
  95 Madison Avenue, New York, NY 10016
  345 Whitney Avenue, New Haven, CT 06511
  5014 West Chester Pike, Edgemont, PA 19028

Introduction © 1987 by Harold Bloom

Printed and bound in the United States of America

∞ The paper used in this publication meets the minimum requirements
of the American National Standard for Permanence of Paper for Printed
Library Materials, Z39.48-1984.

Library of Congress Cataloging-in-Publication Data

Laurence Sterne's Tristram Shandy.

  (Modern critical interpretations)
  Includes index.
  Summary: A collection of seven critical essays on Sterne's novel "The
Life and Opinions of Tristram Shandy, Gent." arranged in chronological
order of publication.
  1. Sterne, Laurence, 1713–1768. Life and opinions of Tristram
Shandy. [1. Sterne, Laurence, 1713–1768. Life and opinions of Tristram
Shandy. 2. English literature—History and criticism] I. Bloom, Harold.
II. Series.
PR3714.L38   1987   823'.6   87–6367
ISBN 0–87754–423–9 (alk. paper)

Contents

Editor's Note / vii

Introduction / 1
   HAROLD BLOOM

On *Tristram Shandy* / 7
   DOROTHY VAN GHENT

Art and Nature: The Duality of Man / 23
   MARTIN PRICE

The Subversion of Satire / 31
   RONALD PAULSON

The Comic Syntax of *Tristram Shandy* / 43
   IAN WATT

Sterne: The Poetics of Sensibility / 59
   MARTIN BATTESTIN

Sterne and the Nostalgia for Reality / 87
   ROBERT ALTER

Sterne and Swift: Augustan Continuities / 107
   MAX BYRD

Chronology / 123

Contributors / 125

Bibliography / 127

Acknowledgments / 131

Index / 133

Editor's Note

This book gathers together a representative selection of the best modern critical essays on Laurence Sterne's *The Life and Opinions of Tristram Shandy, Gent.* The essays are reprinted here in the chronological order of their original publication. I am grateful to Christina Büchmann for her learned assistance in researching this volume.

My introduction centers upon Sterne's intensely dualistic version of Sensibility. Dorothy Van Ghent begins the chronological sequence of criticism with her overview of the novel's "Cervantic humour," both Quixotic and properly low, in the mode of Sancho Panza. The classic exposition of Sterne's dualism, by Martin Price, teaches us that "his satire is moral, but his comedy is epistemological."

Ronald Paulson, one of our major contemporary scholars of satire, emphasizes how Sterne subverts "the conventions not only of Richardson but of Swift and Fielding as well." Shandean laughter, Tristram's comic syntax, is the subject of Ian Watt, historian of the rise of the novel. In an intricate investigation of the poetics of Sensibility in *Tristram Shandy,* Martin Battestin affirms Sterne's belief "that the way out of the self is through the senses."

Robert Alter stresses that Sterne's strange procedures work against novelistic narration "without ever really abandoning the enterprise of the novelist." In this book's final essay, Max Byrd seeks to find a way back to a benign account of literary influence, by attempting to demonstrate the continuities between Swift's *A Tale of a Tub* and *Tristram Shandy.* I would rejoin that no more creative misreading of *A Tale of a Tub* than *Tristram Shandy* is conceivable, at least by me.

Introduction

I

Sterne remarked, in a letter, that *Tristram Shandy* "was made and formed to baffle all criticism," but he probably knew better. Dr. Johnson, greatest of critics, insisted that *Tristram Shandy* would not last, a hopelessly wrong prophecy. Sterne gives the critic and reader everything to do, and can anyone resist, one wonders, a novel in which the hero-narrator declares (volume 1, chapter 14) that "I have been at it these six weeks, making all the speed I possibly could, — and am not yet born"? Published in nine short volumes from 1760 to 1767, *Tristram Shandy* is the masterpiece of what Northrop Frye has taught us to call the Age of Sensibility, the era of Rousseau, and of a secularized, vernacular, "Orientalized" Bible, described by Bishop Lowth (*Lectures on the Sacred Poetry of the Hebrews,* 1753) as the true source of the "language of the passions." It is also the era of John Locke, much as we still live in the Age of Sigmund Freud. Johnson, who also opposed the poetry of Thomas Gray and of his own personal friend, William Collins, was quite consistent in setting himself against *Tristram Shandy.* Henry Fielding may have subverted novelistic forms, but Sterne subverts the entire Augustan mode of representation and truly ends the cultural enterprise in which Pope had triumphed.

It cannot be accidental that so many of the best contemporary Spanish-American novels are Shandean, whether or not the particular writer actually has read Sterne. One such distinguished novelist, when told by me how grand a fantasist he seemed, amiably assured me that his intentions were merely realistic. In the presence of extraordinary actuality, Wallace Stevens observed, consciousness could take the place of imagination. For Sterne, consciousness itself was the extraordinary actuality, so that sensibility became one with imagination. Dualism, Cartesian and Lockean, comes to us now mostly in Freudian guise. "Shandean guise" would do as well, since Sterne is a thorough-

1

going Freudian five generations before Freud. The fundamental Freudian frontier concepts — the drive, the bodily ego, the nonrepressive defenses of introjection and projection — are conceptually exemplified in *Tristram Shandy,* as is the central Freudian idea or trope of repression or defense. Most readers of Sterne see this at once, and many of his critics have reflected upon it. A Freudian exegesis of *Tristram Shandy* therefore becomes a redundancy. Far more vital is the question: What is Sterne trying to do for himself, as a novelist, by his dualistic, solipsistic, psychological emphasis?

That there is an aesthetic and moral program in the Shandean philosophy, most critics agree, but phrasing it has led to some unfortunate banalities. You can sum up Pope's or Fielding's designs upon the reader rather more easily than you can express Sterne's. This is not simply a rhetorical dilemma; Sterne is a great ironist and parodist, but so are Pope and Fielding, while Swift excels even Sterne in such modes. But if all three of the great Augustans are cognitively subtle, Sterne is preternaturally subtle, to the point of being daemonic. Swift is ferocious, yet Sterne is uncanny; his artistry is indeed diabolic as Martin Price comments, comparing it to the skill of Ionesco. The spirit of the comparison is right, but Ionesco hardly can work on Sterne's scale, which is both vast and minute. I prefer Richard Lanham's comparison of Sterne to Chaucer, who also is too wise to fall into an Arnoldian high seriousness. Like Chaucer and Cervantes, Sterne is very serious about play, but he is even more playful about form than they are.

II

What is love, to an almost perfect solipsist? Can it be more than sex? Is sex all, and does every trembling hand make us squeak, like dolls, the wished-for word? Sterne is reductive enough to muse on the question, and to intimate an affirmative answer:

> I had escaped, continued the corporal, all that time from falling in love, and had gone on to the end of the chapter, had it not been predestined otherwise — there is no resisting our fate.
> It was on a *Sunday,* in the afternoon, as I told your honour —
> The old man and his wife had walked out —
> Every thing was still and hush as midnight about the house —
> There was not so much as a duck or a duckling about the yard —
> — When the fair *Beguine* came in to see me.
> My wound was then in a fair way of doing well — the inflammation had been gone off for some time, but it was succeeded

with an itching both above and below my knee, so insufferable, that I had not shut my eyes the whole night for it.

Let me see it, said she, kneeling down upon the ground parallel to my knee, and laying her hand upon the part below it — It only wants rubbing a little, said the *Beguine;* so covering it with the bed cloaths, she began with the fore-finger of her right-hand to rub under my knee, guiding her fore-finger backwards and forwards by the edge of the flannel which kept on the dressing.

In five or six minutes I felt slightly the end of the second finger — and presently it was laid flat with the other, and she continued rubbing in that way round and round for a good while; it then came into my head, that I should fall in love — I blush'd when I saw how white a hand she had — I shall never, an' please your honour, behold another hand so white whilst I live —

— Not in that place: said my uncle *Toby* —

Though it was the most serious despair in nature to the corporal — he could not forbear smiling.

The young *Beguine,* continued the corporal, perceiving it was of great service to me — from rubbing, for some time, with two fingers — proceeded to rub at length, with three — till by little and little she brought down the fourth, and then rubb'd with her whole hand: I will never say another word, an' please your honour, upon hands again — but it was softer than satin —

— Prithee, *Trim,* commend it as much as thou wilt, said my uncle *Toby;* I shall hear thy story with the more delight — The corporal thank'd his master most unfeignedly; but having nothing to say upon the *Beguine*'s hand, but the same over again — he proceeded to the effects of it.

The fair *Beguine,* said the corporal, continued rubbing with her whole hand under my knee — till I fear'd her zeal would weary her — "I would do a thousand times more," said she, "for the love of Christ" — In saying which she pass'd her hand across the flannel, to the part above my knee, which I had equally complained of, and rubb'd it also.

I perceived, then, I was beginning to be in love —

As she continued rub-rub-rubbing — I felt it spread from under her hand, an' please your honour, to every part of my frame —

The more she rubb'd, and the longer strokes she took — the more the fire kindled in my veins — till at length, by two or three strokes longer than the rest — my passion rose to the highest pitch——I seiz'd her hand——

——And then, thou clapped'st it to thy lips, *Trim,* said my uncle *Toby*——and madest a speech.

Whether the corporal's amour terminated precisely in the way my uncle *Toby* described it, is not material; it is enough that it contain'd in it the essence of all the love-romances which ever have been wrote since the beginning of the world. (8, 22)

To be in love is to be aroused; no more, no less. Sterne, something of an invalid, was abnormally sensitive, as W. B. C. Watkins remarked, "——partly because he was inevitably self-conscious physically to an abnormal degree. He was acutely aware of the very circulation of his blood and the beating of his heart." Much of Sterne's alleged prurience is actually his heightened vulnerability, cognitive and bodily, to sexual stimuli. The sense of "Sensibility" in Sterne is fully sexual, and aids us in seeing the true nature of the cultural term, both morally and aesthetically. A susceptibility to tender feelings, however fine, and whether one's own or those of others, becomes objectified as a quality or stance that turns away from the Stoic and Augustan ideal of reason in affective response. This is Sensibility or "the Sentimental" ideologically free from either right-wing celebration of bourgeois morality or left-wing idealization or proletarian or pastoral natural virtues. Its politics, though Whiggish in origin, diffuse into a universal and histrionic vision of the force and beauty of the habits of the heart. Martin Price terms it "a vehement, often defiant assertion of the value of man's feelings." Overtly self-conscious and dramatic, yet insisting upon its sincerity, the stance of Sensibility is a kind of sexualization of all the other effects, as Sterne most clearly knew, showed, and told. Richard Lanham sums this up when he writes that "For Sterne, we finally become not only insatiable pleasure-seekers but, by our nature, incurable poseurs."

All Shandeans have their favorite episodes, and I am tempted to cite all of volume 7, throughout which Tristram/Sterne flees from Death by taking a Sentimental journey through France. One could vote for the story of Amandus and Amanda, or for the concluding country-dance with Nanette, two superb moments in volume 7. But, if we are pleasure-seeking poseurs, we cannot do better than chapter 15 of volume 8, which precedes the Widow Wadman's direct attempt to light Uncle Toby at both ends at once, in the sentry-box:

It is a great pity——but 'tis certain from every day's observation of man, that he may be set on fire like a candle, at either end—— provided there is a sufficient wick standing out; if there is not

——there's an end of the affair; and if there is——by lighting it at the bottom, as the flame in that case has the misfortune generally to put out itself——there's an end of the affair again.

For my part, could I always have the ordering of it which way I would be burnt myself——for I cannot bear the thoughts of being burnt like a beast——I would oblige a housewife constantly to light me at the top; for then I should burn down decently to the socket; that is, from my head to my heart, from my heart to my liver, from my liver to my bowels, and so on by the meseraick veins and arteries, through all the turns and lateral insertions of the intestines and their tunicles to the blind gut——

——I beseech you, doctor *Slop*, quoth my uncle *Toby*, interrupting him as he mentioned the *blind gut*, in a discourse with my father the night my mother was brought to bed of me——I beseech you, quoth my uncle *Toby*, to tell me which is the blind gut; for, old as I am, I vow I do not know to this day where it lies.

The *blind gut*, answered doctor *Slop*, lies betwixt the *Illion* and *Colon*——

——In a man? said my father.

——'Tis precisely the same, cried doctor *Slop*, in a woman—— That's more than I know; quoth my father. (8, 15)

We confront again Sterne's marvelous sense of the dualistic perplexities of human existence. Man is not exactly the Puritan candle of the Lord, burning with a preternatural will-to-holiness, but a sexual candle altogether, burning with the natural will-to-live. When Tristram/Sterne asks to be lit at the top, presumably with cognitive fire, then he asks also to "burn down decently to the socket." Sterne's fierce metaphor rejects the Cartesian ghost-in-the-machine (Gilbert Ryle's fine formulation) and desires instead a conflagration of the mind through the senses. Though he is perhaps the most satirical of all vitalists, Sterne's final affinities seem to be with Rabelais and Blake, visionaries who sought to redeem us through an improvement in sensual enjoyment.

On *Tristram Shandy*

Dorothy Van Ghent

In Sterne's deceptively frivolous, deceptively ingenuous novel *Tristram Shandy,*
a new type of structure makes its appearance, a type that is of singular importance for the development of the modern novel. This is a structure modeled
on the operative character of consciousness as such. Sterne conceives the
behavior of consciousness in terms not of logical continuities but of the spontaneous association of ideas. The word "structure" implies controlled form
and a unity, and it would seem that mere association of one thing with another
could issue in nothing but haphazard multiplicity. Sterne's interest, however,
is that of a novelist and not that of a theoretical psychologist. That is, his
concern is to create a world. The world that he creates has the form of a
mind. It may perhaps help us to grasp the notion of a structure of this sort
if we think of the mind in the figure of one of Leibniz's monads, those elemental units of energy that have "mirrors but no windows": the mirroring
capacity of the unit makes of it a microcosm of the universe, in that all things
are reflected in it; and yet, because it lacks "windows," it is a discrete world
in itself, formally defined only by internal relationships; while the reflections
in its "mirrors" have a free energetic interplay unique for this monad—this
mind—differentiating it from all others at the same time that it is representative of all others.

The novelty of the method employed in *Tristram Shandy* becomes striking as we review the other novels we have read in terms of the importance
of action or plot as an organizing factor in each, and as we consider the relative
unimportance of plot in *Tristram Shandy. Don Quixote* and *The Pilgrim's Progress*
trace the episodes in a hero's quest or mission; the hero goes somewhere to

From *The English Novel: Form and Function.* © 1953 by Dorothy Van Ghent. Harper & Row, 1953.

do something or find something, and the manifest concrete substance of these books lies in the actions he engages in along the way. Similarly, *Moll Flanders* is plotted upon a series of episodic actions, the whole held together formally as Moll's biography. With *Clarissa Harlowe* and *Tom Jones,* action takes on a more unitary—as distinguished from episodic—character: the action of the one book (at least as conceived by Richardson) is that of tragic drama, the action of the other that of comic drama, and obviously both books are unthinkable except with reference to plot complication, reversal, and denouement. What is the "action" of *Tristram Shandy?*

Presumably, like that of *Moll Flanders,* it is episodic and biographical: *The Life and Opinions of Tristram Shandy, Gent.* is the full title. But Tristram is not born until a third of the way through the book; not christened until fifty pages later; the story is more than half over when we are told that he has reached the age of five (scarcely yet the age for "opinions"); is two-thirds finished by the time he is put into breeches; suddenly he appears as a gentleman on his travels in France; and the novel ends with an episode that concerns not Tristram but Uncle Toby. Those sporadic flickers of narrative in which Tristram is seen in chronological circumstance as the hero-in-action (if the hero *can* be thought of as "acting" while he is being born, christened, circumcised, etc.) evidently do not serve the same purposes of narrative that we have observed elsewhere; they are, rather, if they are anything, an intentional mockery of "action." Chronological and plot continuity are, then, not definitively organizational to *Tristram Shandy.* The fact appears extraordinary when we stop for a moment to consider how naturally, habitually, almost stubbornly we tend to think of all experience as somehow automatically dished up to us, like a molded pudding, in the form of chronology; and how this tendency to see experience as actions related to each other undisturbedly by the stages of the clock and the calendar leads us to expect of fiction that it will provide a similar unidirectional action, or series of episodes, taking place chronologically. *Tristram Shandy* pays lip service to this expectation— at least by allowing Tristram to be born before he is christened, to be put into breeches before he goes traveling in France—but so mockingly as to make us aware that Sterne is engaged in deliberate demolition of chronological sequences and (inasmuch as our notions of "time" and "action" are inextricably related) deliberate destruction of the common notion of "action."

But this is the negative aspect only, and if this were all there were to Sterne's concern with the relationship of time and human experience, then the squiggly lines he draws in chapter 40 of book 6, to show the haphazard progress of his novel, could represent just that: its haphazardness, its lack of form. But it is anything but haphazard or formless. Obeying formal laws of its own, it is as skillfully and delicately constructed as *Tom Jones*. Having ruled out plot chronology as a model of the way experience presents itself, Sterne offers another model: that of the operations of consciousness, where time is exploded, where any time-past may be time-present, or several times-past be concurrently present at once, and where clock-time appears only intermittently as a felt factor. As Cervantes's *Don Quixote* offers fiction as many models as it can use, so it offers this one also. In the episode of Quixote's descent into the cave of Montesinos, the time of dream and of poetry, the ancient heroic time of Montesinos and Durandarte, the modern time of coinage and "new dimity petticoats," and the actual hours of the descent and of the Knight's sleep, merge as one time.

But what is to give unity to this model, if we cannot plot the hero's adventures on clock and calendar in order to know when they begin and when they are ended, and if we do not, after all, have a hero to "act" in the ordinary sense—no time, no hero, no action? The unity of any novel may be described on several different levels; we may speak of the unifying function of theme, or of plot, or of symbolism, or of other elements that appear to have superior importance. The total structural unity of a work does not yield itself to a simple description, but only to a quite lengthy analysis of the complex interrelationships of all major elements. At the most conspicuous level, the unity of *Tristram Shandy* is the unity of Tristram's—the narrator's—consciousness. This is a representative kind of unity, psychologically true to the way in which experience appears to all of us to have its most rudimentary unity; for though clock-time may seem to cut experience into units, these are arbitrary units that melt into each other unrecognizably in the individual's self-feeling; and though we may assume that a shared experience has a certain definite, common form and description for those who share it, yet we know that, as the experience is absorbed into and transformed by the individual consciousness, it is something very different for different people, and that its form and "oneness" or unity are felt most concretely only as the experience is stamped by the character of the individual consciousness.

Sterne's project in *Tristram Shandy* was not to have a parallel, in the work of a major novelist, until Proust wrote *Remembrance of Things Past*. Though each of these books, so far separated in time and in local culture, carries the highly singular and special flavor of its historical circumstances and of the original genius of its author, they have a strong kinship in subject and plan and quality. Each makes of the narrator's consciousness its subject matter; the artistry of each lies in the "objectifying" of this "subjective" material in its own right and for its own sake, so that the "subjective" becomes an object to be manipulated and designed and given aesthetic form according to laws inherent in it; and each creates an Alice-in-Wonderland world that is unique and inimitable because the individual consciousness is itself unique and inimitable. We do not think of Proust's work as the story of Swann, or the story of Charlus or of Albertine or even of Marcel, or as the history of a transmogrification of social classes and manners in the late nineteenth century, although it is these and other stories and histories as well. Nor do we think of *Tristram Shandy* as a series of character sketches of Uncle Toby and Walter Shandy and Corporal Trim and the Widow Wadman, or as a mosaic of sentimental and slapstick anecdotes, some gracefully pathetic, some uproarious, and all peppered with off-color puns and double entendres, the indulgences of a neurotic clergyman—although it is these and still other things. We think of *Tristram Shandy,* as we do of Proust's *Remembrance of Things Past,* as a mind in which the local world has been steeped and dissolved and fantastically re-formed, so that it issues brand new. Still more definitive of the potentialities of Sterne's method, as these have been realized in a great modern work, is James Joyce's *Finnegans Wake,* where the hero's dream swallows and recomposes all time in its belly of mirrors, and where the possibilities lying in Sterne's creative play with linguistic associations—his use of language as a dynamic system in itself, a magic system for the "raising" of new perceptions as a magician's formulas "raise" spirits—are enormously developed. Joyce himself points out the parallel. In the second paragraph of *Finnegans Wake,* "Sir Tristram, violer d'amores," arrives from over the sea "to wielderfight his penisolate war" in "Laurens County," and we know—among these puns—that we are not in wholly unfamiliar territory.

Sterne's project, like Proust's, was to analyze and represent in his novel the creative process; and that Sterne should be the first practitioner of what is called the technique of the "stream of consciousness" in fictional writing is consonant with the kind of subject he set himself. Our fictional center of gravity is not a happening or confluence of happenings nor a character or concourse of characters under emotional or moral or social aspects of interest; it consists rather in the endlessly fertile rhythms of a consciousness, as those rhythms explore the comic ironies of a quest for order among the humdrum freaks of birth and paternity and place and time and language. In reading *Tristram Shandy,* we are never allowed to forget that the activity of creation, as an activity of forming perceptions and maneuvering them into an expressive order, *is itself the subject;* the technique does not allow us to forget it—for let alone the harum-scarum tricks with printer's ink, the narrator plunges at us in apostrophes, flirts his addresses at us with "Dear Sir" or "Dear Madam," explodes into the middle of a disquisition or a scene in defiance of time, space, and logic. Uncle Toby, pursuing the theory of projectiles in the pages of half a dozen military authors, becomes involved among parabolas, parameters, semiparameters, conic sections, and angles of incidence, and Tristram suddenly cries out,

> O my uncle; — fly — fly, fly from it as from a serpent . . . Alas!
> 'twill exasperate thy symptoms, — check thy perspirations —
> evaporate thy spirits — waste thy animal strength, — dry up thy
> radical moisture, bring thee into a costive habit of body, — impair
> thy health, — and hasten all the infirmities of thy old age. — O
> my uncle! my uncle Toby.

Toby's investigations were conducted some years before Tristram was born. It is as if Tristram were sitting in a moving-picture theater, watching on a most candid and intimate screen the performance of his progenitors. He is struck suddenly with admiration or consternation, stands up, waves his arms, applauds, boos, wrings his hands, sheds tears, sits down and tickles the lady next to him.

We have said that the unity of *Tristram Shandy* is the unity of the narrator's consciousness; but — without the discipline afforded by chronology, or an objective "narrative line," or a moral thesis of some sort — what is the principle of selection by which the contents of that consciousness present themselves? Sterne himself puts the question, in chapter 23, book 3, and as he states it, it is the problem of every novelist. In setting up a certain body of human experience novelistically, what should come first? what last? what should follow or precede what? Should not everything appear at once and in fusion, inasmuch as this is the way the author's consciousness grasps it in its fullest truth? But the novel itself is an artifact subjected to time law; words follow words and pages follow pages in temporal sequence, necessarily imposing temporal sequence upon the material; everything cannot be said at once, although this disability may seem to injure the wholeness and instantaneousness of the material as the author grasps it. Trim announces to Toby that Dr. Slop is in the kitchen making a bridge. " 'Tis very obliging in him," Toby says, mistaking the bridge (meant for Tristram's nose) for a drawbridge. The author must elucidate Toby's error; but when? Right now, at the moment Toby makes the remark? But the goings-on upstairs in Mrs. Shandy's bedchamber are of the greatest consequence now. Later, then, among the anecdotes of Toby's amours with Widow Wadman? Or in the middle of Toby's campaigns on the bowling green? All of these circumstances press upon the author at once, and are, in the atemporal time of consciousness, contemporaneous. By what principle of selection is he to subject them to the time demands of the novel?

> O ye powers! [Sterne cries] . . . which enable mortal man to tell a story worth the hearing — that kindly shew him, where he is to begin it — and where he is to end it — what he is to put into it — and what he is to leave out — . . .
>
> I beg and beseech you . . . that wherever in any part of your dominions it so falls out, that three several roads meet in one point, as they have done just here — that at least you set up a guide-post in the centre of them, in mere charity, to direct an uncertain devil which of the three he is to take.

Sterne's uncertainty is not really uncertainty at all. His cry of authorial distress is one of the many false scents he lays down humoristically in order to give to his work the appearance of artlessness and primitive spontaneity. At the same time it points up the paradox of all novel writing, the paradox of which Sterne is very much aware: the antagonism between the time sequences which the novel imposes, and the instantaneous wholeness of the image of complex human experience which the novel attempts to present. Sterne has his guidepost in the philosopher John Locke, and it is according to Locke's theory of the human understanding that he finds his way down all the several roads that are continuously meeting in one point in *Tristram Shandy*, or, conversely, we might say that it is with the guidance of Locke that he contrives continually to get his roads crossed. To the French Academician, M. Suard, he said in conversation that "those who knew the philosopher (Locke) well enough to recognize his presence and his influence would find them or sense them on every page, in every line." Locke had attempted to explain the genesis of ideas from sensation. Simple sensations produce simple ideas of those sensations; associated sensations produce associated ideas of sensations, a process which becomes immensely complicated with the accretion of other associations of this kind. Besides the capacity of the mind to form ideas from sensations, it has the capacity of reflection. By reflection upon ideas acquired from sensation, it is able to juggle these into new positions and relationships, forming what we call "abstract ideas." Thus the whole body of logical and inferential "knowledge" is built up, through association, from the simple primary base of sensation. There are two aspects of this theory which are of chief importance in Sterne. The one is the Sensational aspect, the other the Associative. From the notion of sensation as the prime source of knowledge and as the primitive character of experience, arises that doctrine of "sensibility" or "sentimentality" which Sterne made famous: the doctrine that value lies in *feeling* as such. With this we shall concern ourselves later. But at this point let us see how the associative aspect of Locke's theory appears structurally in *Tristram Shandy.*

Tristram starts out on the first page with a disquisition on the need of parents to mind what they are about when they are in the act of begetting. Why? Because their associated sensations at that moment have a determining effect upon the nature and destiny of Homunculus. (Note the manner in which, from the beginning, Sterne's imagination *concretizes* an abstraction, here an abstraction of eugenical theory: the "humours and dispositions which were then uppermost" in father and mother suffuse, somewhat like a glandular tincture, the "animal spirits" passed on to the son; and the metaphor hinted by "animal spirits" becomes instantly a picture of unharnessed horses — "Away they go cluttering like hey-go mad." This concreteness of imagination is one of the secrets of Sterne's surprises and of the Alice-in-Wonderland character of his world, for it is with a shock of astonished and delighted recognition that we suddenly see the pedantic abstraction taken literally and transformed into physiology, complete with hooves, feathers, or haberdashery.) What went wrong with Tristram's begetting was that Mrs. Shandy, accustomed to associate the winding of the clock with the marital act (like Pavlov's dogs and the dinner bell), missed the association appropriate at the moment, and in speaking of it to Mr. Shandy distracted his attention and prepared for poor Homunculus nine long months of disordered nerves and melancholy dreams (a pre-Freudian comment on the assumed bliss of this period). Mrs. Shandy's remark about the clock leads then, by association of ideas, to a portrait of Uncle Toby, typically "wiping away a tear"; for it was to Uncle Toby that Tristram owed the information as to the circumstances of his begetting. Again, by association with conception, origin, *the egg,* we are led, in chapter 4, into a discussion of Horace's dictum on the technique of beginning a literary work: "as Horace says, *ab Ovo*" — which Horace did not say but which nevertheless serves as an apology for Sterne's own technique; thence to an explanation of Mrs. Shandy's unfortunate association between the winding of the clock and the marital act — "Which strange combination of ideas," says Sterne,

> the sagacious Locke, who certainly understood the nature of these things better than most men, affirms to have produced more wry actions than all other sources of prejudice whatsoever.

The explanation leads to a determination of the date of Tristram's geniture and the manner of his birth, which involves a digression into the history of the midwife, which in turn involves a digression into the history of the

parson Yorick, who was responsible for establishing the midwife in her voca-
tion; and the history of Yorick necessitates first a description of his horse
(before we can get back to the midwife), but the parson's horse recalls
Rosinante, and that steed, that belonged to a famous gentleman with a hobby,
sets Sterne off on the subject of hobbyhorses in general, which leads
to . . . (When are we going to learn the circumstances of Tristram's birth?)
Sterne's comment on "the sagacious Locke," who understood the "strange
combination of ideas" to which men's brains are liable, indicates the method
here. It is precisely in the *strangeness* of the combinations or associations that
Sterne finds the contour of his subject, the logic of its grotesquerie and the
logic of its gaiety. At the same time, he is in perfect control of the "combinations," as we are slyly reminded again and again; for we *do* come back
to the midwife.

Nor, in terms of total structure, is Mrs. Shandy's remark about the clock,
in the first chapter, quite as irresponsible as it would seem. In this odd world,
where the methodical Mr. Shandy winds up the house clock, together with
"some other little family concernments," on the first Sunday night of every
month, time is of the utmost importance and the utmost unimportance. Let
us illustrate. In chapter 9 of book 4, Toby and Mr. Shandy are conversing
as they walk down the stairs, and from chapter 9 to chapter 14 we are kept,
presumably, in the chronological span that covers their descent from the top
to the bottom of the staircase. Chapter 9 starts out,

> What a chapter of chances, said my father, turning himself about
> upon the first landing, as he and my uncle Toby were going
> downstairs—

and there follows a page of conversation between the two. With the beginning of chapter 10, Sterne reminds us that we are still on the staircase and
have not got to the bottom yet.

> Is it not a shame to make two chapters of what passed in going
> down one pair of stairs? for we are got no farther yet than to
> the first landing, and there are fifteen more steps down to the
> bottom; and for aught I know, as my father and my uncle Toby
> are in a talking humour, there may be as many chapters as
> steps: . . .

a remark which obviously calls for the insertion here of his "chapter upon
chapters" (which he has promised us, along with his chapter on noses, his
chapter on knots, and his chapter on whiskers). Hence, by chapter 11, we
are not yet to the bottom of the staircase.

We shall bring all things to rights, said my father, setting his foot upon the first step from the landing. ——

With chapter 12, Susannah appears below.

> —— And how does your mistress? cried my father, taking the same step over again from the landing, and calling to Susannah, whom he saw passing by the foot of the stairs with a huge pin-cushion in her hand —— how does your mistress? As well, said Susannah, tripping by, but without looking up, as can be expected. —— What a fool am I! said my father, drawing his leg back again —— let things be as they will, brother Toby, 'tis ever the precise answer —— And how is the child, pray? —— No answer. And where is Dr. Slop? added my father, raising his voice aloud, and looking over the ballusters —— Susannah was out of hearing.
>
> Of all the riddles of a married life, said my father, crossing the landing in order to set his back against the wall, whilst he propounded it to my uncle Toby —— of all the puzzling riddles. . . .

In chapter 13, Sterne desperately appeals to the critic to step in and get Uncle Toby and Mr. Shandy off the stairs for him. Obviously, what has been presented to us in this bit of fantasy is the incongruity between the clock-time which it will take to get the two conversationalists down the stairs, and the atemporal time—the "timeless time"—of the imagination, where the words of Toby and Mr. Shandy echo in their plenitude, where their stances and gestures are traced in precise images (as a leg is lifted or a foot withdrawn from the step), and where also the resonances of related subjects (such as chance and chapters and critics) intertwine freely with the conversation of Toby and Walter; and we are made aware of the paradox of which Sterne is so actively aware, and which he uses as a selective principle and as a structural control: the paradox of man's existence both in time and out of time—his existence in the time of the clock, and his existence in the apparent timelessness of consciousness (what has been called, by philosophers, "duration," to distinguish it from clock-marked time).

But the time fantasy still piles up, in chapter 13, in odder contours. We are reminded, by Walter's interchange with Susannah, that this is the day of Tristram's birth; and the autobiographer Tristram is also suddenly reminded of the passage of time.

> I am this month one whole year older than I was this time twelve-month; and having got, as you perceive, almost into the middle of my fourth volume —— and no farther than to my first day's life ——

—'tis demonstrative that I have three hundred and sixty-four days
more life to write just now, than when I first set out; so that
instead of advancing, as a common writer, in my work with what
I have been doing at it—on the contrary, I am just thrown so
many volumes back . . . at this rate I should just live 364 times
faster than I should write—

—a piece of mathematical calculation which the reader will follow as he is
able. Again, what the fantasy suggests is the paradoxical temporal and yet
atemporal status of consciousness, whose experience is at once past experience,
as marked by the passage of time, and present experience, inasmuch as it
is present within the mind. These considerations of time may seem abstract
as set down here, but we are simplifying Sterne's performance so that we
may see it structurally and schematically. Actually, what his acute time sense
provides is never the dullness and ponderousness of abstraction, but the utmost concreteness of visualization—a concreteness which we have seen in
the descent of Toby and Mr. Shandy down the stairs. Mr. Shandy turns himself
about the first landing; he sets his foot upon the first step from the landing;
he takes the same step over again; he draws his leg back; he looks over the
balusters at Susannah; he crosses the landing to set his back against the wall.
These are Sterne's typical time markings, showing the procession of stance
and gesture, but they are also the delicately observed details of the dramatic
picture, which bring it alive and concrete before our eyes, and which make
of the characters of *Tristram Shandy* creatures who, once known, remain un-
fadingly, joyously vivid to our imagination.

It is because of Sterne's acute awareness of time passage and of the con-
undrums of the time sense, that he is also so acutely aware of the concrete
moment; or, conversely, we could say that it is because of his awareness of
the preciousness of the concrete moment, that he is so acutely aware of time,
which destroys the moment. In the eighth chapter of the final book, he engages
in an apostrophe.

Time wastes too fast: every letter I trace tells me with what rapidity
Life follows my pen; the days and hours of it, more precious,
my dear Jenny! than the rubies about thy neck, are flying over
our heads like light clouds of a windy day, never to return more
—everything presses on—whilst thou art twisting that lock, —
see! it grows grey; and every time I kiss thy hand to bid adieu,
and every absence which follows it, are preludes to that eternal
separation which we are shortly to make. —

Which calls for a new "chapter" of a single line—"Now, for what the world thinks of that ejaculation—I would not give a groat." The philosopher, with his head full of time, is never allowed to sail off into abstraction; he keeps his eye on Jenny twisting her lock. For it is not in abstract speculation about time, but precisely in Jenny's gesture as she twists her lock, that the time sense finds profoundest significance; or in Trim's gesture as he drops his hat on the kitchen floor to illustrate to Obadiah and Susannah the catastrophe of mortal passage into oblivion.

Let us stay with Trim's hat for a moment, for it will illustrate for us another and equally important structural irony in *Tristram Shandy.*

> ——"Are we not here now;" continued the corporal, "and are we not"—(dropping his hat plumb upon the ground——and pausing, before he pronounced the word)——"gone! in a moment?" The descent of the hat was as if a heavy lump of clay had been kneaded into the crown of it.——Nothing could have expressed the sentiment of mortality, of which it was the type and forerunner, like it,——his hand seemed to vanish from under it,——it fell dead,——the corporal's eye fixed upon it, as upon a corpse, ——and Susannah burst into a flood of tears.
>
> Now——ten thousand, and ten thousand times ten thousand (for matter and motion are infinite) are the ways by which a hat may be dropped upon the ground, without any effect.——Had he flung it, or thrown it, or cast it, or skimmed it, or squirted it, or let it slip or fall in any possible direction under heaven, . . . the effect upon the heart had been lost.
>
> Ye who govern this mighty world and its mighty concerns with the engines of eloquence . . . meditate——meditate, I beseech you, upon Trim's hat.

What, of course, gives the scene that incongruity in which humor lies, is the use of Trim's gesture with his hat as a symbol of mortality: that is, the equating of the trivial with the serious, the unimportant with the important. Coleridge, speculating on the "one humorific point common to all that can be called humorous," found that common point to lie in

> a certain reference to the general and the universal, by which the finite great is brought into identity with the little, or the little with the finite great, so as to make both nothing in comparison with the infinite. The little is made great, and the great little, in order to destroy both; because all is equal in contrast with the infinite.

It is indeed Sterne to whom Coleridge immediately refers for illustration of the point. Trim's gesture with his hat is one among innumerable instances in the book. It is the "finite little" brought into identity with the "finite great" (and the references to tens of thousands and the "mighty world" domesticate the "finite great" in the Shandy kitchen and in the even smaller quarters under the crown of Trim's hat), making of both "nothing in comparison with the infinite."

If we are accustomed to think of "humor" as the type of the comic strip, we may feel that Coleridge's definition of humor, and its application to *Tristram Shandy*, are much too serious—too "deep"—to have relevance to the funny. How can we laugh, if our minds are supposed to be oriented to the "finite great" and the "infinite"? It has been said, very wisely, that "comedy is a serious matter"; and though we are not speaking of "comedy" here (for we have reserved this term for dramatic writing of the order of *Tom Jones*, which is constructed on traditional principles of comic drama), but of "humor," we may say that humor, too, is a serious matter. Nor would it be improbable that, in analyzing the source of humor in the best comic strips, the observer would find that Coleridge's definition was applicable. (Needless to say, we do not laugh when we are analytically intent on understanding *why* we laugh. The laughter has come first.) It is a definition of humor that is fertile also for an understanding of certain neglected aspects of modern writers, such as Dostoyevski and Kafka, who, though deeply "serious" writers, are at the same time great humorists; and our understanding of the "seriousness" of Sterne's humor can prepare us for a larger understanding of those authors nearer our time, who are concerned seriously with the problems of our time, but who are sensitive also to the sources of laughter.

Let us take one more passage to illustrate our meaning. We have said that we would need to consider rather more carefully that influential aspect of Locke's theory of the understanding which is its Sensationalism—its grounding of knowledge in sensation—and of Sterne's indebtedness to Locke for his doctrine of "sensibility" or "sentimentality," which measures the value of experience in terms of its feeling-fulness, the experience that is full of feeling ("sensation," "sensibility," "sentiment") being the valuable experience. We shall not take one of the famous "sentimental" passages—such as that concerning Uncle Toby and the fly, or the death of Le Fever. Tristram's encounter with Maria (chapter 24, book 9) will do. What we shall look for here is the equating of "great" and trivial, which resonates in humor because of the strange balance contrived between these incommensurables. Tristram is on his way to Moulins, and hears a flute player on the road.

—They were the sweetest notes I ever heard; and I instantly

let down the fore-glass to hear them more distinctly — 'Tis Maria; said the postillion, observing I was listening — Poor Maria, continued he (leaning his body on one side to let me see her, for he was in a line betwixt us), is sitting upon a bank playing her vespers upon her pipe, with her little goat beside her.

The young fellow utter'd this with an accent and a look so perfectly in tune to a feeling heart, that I instantly made a vow, I would give him a four-and-twenty sous piece, when I got to Moulins —

— And who is poor Maria? said I.

The love and piety of all the villages around us; said the postillion — it is but three years ago, that the sun did not shine upon so fair, so quick-witted and amiable a maid; and better fate did Maria deserve, than to have her Banns forbid, by the intrigues of the curate of the parish who published them —

He was going on, when Maria, who had made a short pause, put the pipe to her mouth, and began the air again — they were the same notes; — yet were ten times sweeter: It is the evening service to the Virgin, said the young man — but who has taught her to play it — or how she came by her pipe, no one knows; we think that heaven has assisted her in both; for ever since she has been unsettled in her mind, it seems her only consolation — she has never once had the pipe out of her hand, but plays that service upon it almost night and day . . .

We had got up by this time almost to the bank where Maria was sitting: she was in a thin white jacket, with her hair, all but two tresses, drawn up into a silk-net, with a few olive leaves twisted a little fantastically on one side — she was beautiful; and if ever I felt the full force of an honest heart-ache, it was the moment I saw her —

This is the adumbration of a pathetic, a "sentimental" story, in the manner of Cervantes's pastorals (and Sterne apostrophizes Cervantes at the beginning of the chapter). What comes under the denomination of the "finite great" in it is the pathos, the communicated feeling or sensation of pity (the postillion speaks "in tune to a feeling heart," and Tristram feels "the full force of an honest heart-ache") over Maria's love tragedy and madness, and the inference of Heaven's interest in her sad career. But the sketch ends suddenly on a different note. Under the spell of Maria's melancholy cadences, Tristram has leaped out of the coach and seated himself beside her on the bank, between Maria and her goat.

> Maria look'd wistfully for some time at me, and then at her goat
> — and then at me — and then at her goat again, and so on,
> alternately —
> — Well, Maria, said I softly — What resemblance do you find?

The typical goatishness here, and the "sportive pattern of alternation" (with
Maria looking at Tristram, then at the goat, then at Tristram — a pattern
which is one of the distinguishing traits of Sterne's style) illustrate that term
of the humorous equation which is the "finite little," the trivial, the whimsical, and which, capping off the full-blowing cumulus of Maria's pathos,
asks finite judgment to suspend its intoxicated action for a moment in a healthy
smile at its own potency for exaggeration, hysteria, and error.

Sterne wrote to a hesitant admirer, who had objected to his detailed
treatment of Dr. Slop's fall in the mud,

> I will reconsider Slops fall & my too Minute Account of it —
> but in general I am persuaded that the happiness of the Cervantic
> humour arises from this very thing — of describing silly and tri-
> fling Events, with the Circumstantial Pomp of great Ones —
> perhaps this is Overloaded — & I can soon ease it.

Happily, he did not "ease it," but left Dr. Slop in full benefit of his original
tumble, "unwiped, unappointed, unannealed." Sterne's insight into the nature
of the humorous situation, as expressed in the letter, is simply the immediate
technical version of Coleridge's later and more philosophical analysis of humor
that we have cited; for to identify the "finite great" with the "finite little"
becomes, in the actual handling of situation, a description of "silly and trifling Events, with the Circumstantial Pomp of Great Ones" — or the converse of this, as in the story of Toby and the fly, where the trifling event
is treated with the grand diction and gesture and the palpitating feeling of
pompous circumstance. Sterne has been taken to task, many times over, for
his indulgence in pruriency, his slips into indecency, his tendency — as in the
story of Maria — to lapse into goatishness and spoil a softly solemn, tear-jerking
story. That he was perfectly capable of writing the tear-jerker is evident,
nor was anyone more aware of this than Sterne. Frequently, one feels, he
must have been tempted to outsentimentalize the sentimentalists, knowing
the delicacy of his hand at the pathetic (as in the story of Le Fever's death).
But his genius was the humorous genius, and he remained faithful to it. What
have been considered his indecent lapses must be taken as an essential element in the whole Sterne, one term of a structural irony, and a provision
for keeping the sentimental and the emotional and the pathetic in the same
human world with the obscene and the trivial and the absurd. His reference,

in the letter quoted above, to the "Cervantic humour" reminds us that the high-minded knight, Quixote, could not continue on his travels without his low companion, Sancho.

Art and Nature: The Duality of Man

Martin Price

Sterne intensifies the casual pattern of ordinary life even more than Fielding, and his characters become the ludicrous victims of rigorously interrelated events. *The Life and Opinions of Tristram Shandy, Gent.* is, among other things, a triumph of the "genetic method." Tristram's character is accounted for by the physical causes that operate upon him from the very moment of conception. With Mrs. Shandy's "unseasonable question" about the clock, "a foundation [has] been laid for a thousand weaknesses both of body and mind"—so that Tristram will "neither think nor act," as his father puts it, "like any other man's child" (bk. 1, chaps. 2–3). The chain of casuality that follows is brilliantly complicated; it reaches back into the history of the Shandy family and forward to the moment at which the book is being written. Walter Shandy's theories and his wife's stubbornness have produced a marriage settlement that exposes Tristram to the forceps of Dr. Slop: "so that I was doom'd, by marriage articles, to have my nose squeez'd as flat to my face, as if the destinies had actually spun me without one," and "a train of vexatious disappointments, in one stage or other of my life, have pursued me from the mere loss, or rather compression, of this one single member" (1, 15). Again, Walter's theory of names requires that his son be called Trismegistus, a name that Susannah the maid cannot master, and so it collapses into Tristram, the name Walter considers the most inauspicious. And the obsession of Toby Shandy with fortifications leads Corporal Trim to melt down for lead all the sash weights he can find, with the result that Tristram is circumcised by the sudden fall of a window—circumcised or worse, as Dr. Slop suggests

From *To the Palace of Wisdom: Studies in Order and Energy from Dryden to Blake.* © 1964 by Martin Price. Southern Illinois University Press, 1964.

in his desire to magnify the value of his treatment. As in *Tom Jones*, events flow from character but not from one responsible hero—rather from several characters brought into what the astrologers once called malign conjunction. And while the rigor of events causes temporary distress to Tom Jones or Sophia Western, here it works calamity upon the small body of Tristram, and upon the "opinions" that will be formed within it. The rigor of causality, the physical form it takes, the helplessness of the infant—all these give a new note to Sterne's novel.

The theme of human ineffectuality runs through all the main characters. The possibility of impotence hovers over all the Shandy males—whether in wounded groins, flattened noses, or a sheer distrust of feeling, like Walter's. But in a larger sense of impotence, Walter's mixture of irritability and love of far-fetched hypotheses produces constant frustration. Toby's shy, slow innocence and love of his game of fortifications keep him securely childlike. And Yorick's refusal to defend himself against slander and suspicion ensures that he will remain a perpetual victim of others' malice or envy. These disabilities of temperament are as crippling as Tristram's physical misadventures, and we see the two becoming one in the temperament of Tristram as author—unable to sustain connected narrative, fantastic and whimsical, emotionally undisciplined, as much the victim as the author of his book.

Or so Sterne pretends. He gives us—in Toby, Walter, and Yorick—curiously reduced versions of the great aspirations of soldier, scholar, and priest. They can, in fact, be seen as versions of the orders of Pascal. One might expect the order of flesh to be embodied in the soldier, but Toby's mildness is the denial of the search for power. His military force arises from tender loyalty, his elaborate operations on the bowling green are an end in themselves—a reduction of warfare to a harmless game, and his readiness to fight in behalf of his country is more than offset by his warm charity. So, too, in Walter we have all the towering structures and lofty rhetoric of the order of mind, but the systems are half-superstitious, half-playful—the harmless obsessions of an eccentric amateur. In Yorick we come to the order of charity, but Yorick's disdain for the world is ruefully ludicrous and self-mocking. The vestiges of greatness adhere to the professions, but not to these men. Tristram shares in their unsuccess. He holds all the orders in ironic perspective, but, unlike the narrator of Fielding's novels, he is not securely ironic. He alternates between defiance and deception, appeal and assault. He is intensely histrionic, as if he knew that none of the roles he assumes may be sustained for very long at a time, that none in itself will suffice, that the very shifting of roles is necessary to the full act of awareness.

Throughout his work Sterne plays off the crippled body or temperament, seen from the outside as the ludicrous victim of circumstance, with the expansive mind, which tries to convert all it apprehends into the stuff of its obsessions. We see this most clearly in Toby, who is baffled by words and tortured by the difficulty of handling maps until he hits upon the expedient of recreating his vision on the bowling green. There he builds, in small scale, the world in which his mind lives. It is a world he can control and reshape at will, and all the furniture of the larger and less real world about him (notably the sash weights of young Tristram's nursery window) is transformed into the gear of his imaginary battlefield. There warfare becomes a pure tactical game, abstracted from cruelty and suffering. The innocuousness of the game helps to set the scale, as with the game of ombre in Pope's *Rape of the Lock*, but the game is also the perfect vehicle for obsession—complex, absorbing, and self-contained.

Walter's mind expands into hypothesis. "It is the nature of an hypothesis, when once a man has conceived it, that it assimilates every thing to itself as proper nourishment; and, from the first moment of your begetting it, it generally grows the stronger by every thing you see, hear, read, or understand" (2, 19). And Walter, like the spider in Swift's *Battle of the Books,* has a horror of anything—whether the intrusion of stubborn fact or the exposure of miscalculation—that will destroy his fabric: "error, Sir, creeps in thro' the minute holes, and small crevices, which human nature leaves unguarded" (2, 19). Walter's predilection for seeing things "in his own light," "out of the high-way of thinking," makes his intellectual systems as self-contained and obsessive as Toby's game. Walter is so tenacious in his opinions, we are told, that he "would intrench and fortify them round with as many circumvallations and breastworks, as my uncle *Toby* would a citadel" (3, 34).

In a more general way, Walter is infatuated with words. When he discovers, for the sake of his son, a "North-west passage to the intellectual world" through the mastery of auxiliary verbs, we see a brilliant reduction of all his ambitions to their essence. The use of auxiliary verbs, he tells Yorick, "is, at once to set the soul a going by herself upon the materials as they are brought her; and by the versability of this great engine, round which they are twisted, to open new tracks of enquiry, and make every idea engender millions" (5, 42). And Walter triumphantly builds his world of words:

A WHITE BEAR! Very well. Have I ever seen one? Might I ever have seen one? Am I ever to see one? Ought I ever to have seen one? Or can I ever see one?

Would I had seen a white bear! (for how can I imagine it?)

If I should see a white bear, what should I say? If I should never see a white bear, what then?

If I never have, can, must or shall see a white bear alive; have

> I ever seen the skin of one? Did I ever see one painted? —
> described? Have I never dreamed of one?
>   Did my father, mother, uncle, aunt, brothers or sisters, ever
> see a white bear? What would they give? How would they behave?
> How would the white bear have behaved? Is he wild? Tame?
> Terrible? Rough? Smooth? (5, 43)

Like the priests of Pope's Dulness or the ebullient Conrad Crambe of the
Memoirs of Scriblerus, Walter has succeeded in confining the mind to words
alone.

The conflicts that inevitably ensue between rival obsessions are like the
sudden confrontation of two rival orders that meet in a common term. There
can, it is true, be moments of communication. When Trim mistakes Walter's
auxiliaries for troops, Toby, for once, can see the error: "The auxiliaries,
Trim, my brother is talking about, — I conceive to be different things."
Even Walter is astonished. "You do? said my father, rising up" (5, 42). Toby's
customary role is to switch the train of ideas from the track of Walter's obsessions to his own; he does it guilelessly enough, for he cannot credit the reality of Walter's world enough to sense the difference. This comedy of incomprehension can become very complicated, as comedy tends to do. After his
son Bobby's death, Walter reads aloud Servius Simplicius's consolatory letter
to Cicero, with its references to travels in Asia (where Walter had once gone
as a merchant). Toby takes the letter as Walter's own and asks when it was
written. "Simpleton! said my father — 'twas forty years before Christ was
born." Toby's warm sympathy is aroused; he is convinced that Walter is
maddened by grief, and he prays silently for his brother with tears in his
eyes. And Walter, in turn, is pleased with the tears, which he takes as a
tribute to his moving delivery (5, 3).

The most startling and brilliant treatment of this comedy of the mind
locking itself up in its own world is Trim's reading of Yorick's sermon. Trim's
brother Tom has been a captive of the Inquisition for fourteen years, and
as Trim reads the sermon — with its images of the Inquisition's victims — all
distance between himself and the world he is evoking breaks down:

> "To be convinced of this, go with me for a moment into the prisons
> of the inquisition." — [God help my poor brother *Tom*.] —
> "Behold *Religion*, and *Mercy* and *Justice* chained down under her
> feet, — there sitting ghastly upon a black tribunal, propp'd up
> with racks and instruments of torment. Hark! — hark! what a
> piteous groan." [Here *Trim's* face turned as pale as ashes.] "See
> the melancholy wretch who utter'd it," — [Here the tears began

to trickle down] "just brought forth to undergo the anguish of a mock trial, and endure the utmost pains that a studied system of cruelty has been able to invent." — [D — n them all, quoth *Trim*, his colour returning into his face as red as blood.] — "Behold this helpless victim delivered up to his tormentors, — his body so wasted with sorrow and confinement." — [Oh! 'tis my brother, cried poor *Trim* in a most passionate exclamation, dropping the sermon upon the ground, and clapping his hands together — I fear 'tis poor *Tom*]. (2, 17)

Even when Trim cannot go on with his reading and Walter takes over, Trim cannot bear to leave. Trim's is a case of ludicrous obsession and yet of admirable intensity of feeling. His power of sympathy breaks through all the forms of language and achieves a terrifying immediacy. The pathology of his response is clear enough: in its naive form, it is the child's cry of warning at the play; and in its more obsessive form, it is the sending of letters and gifts to fictional characters of television programs. Trim shows us the folly of the obsessive imagination, but since his obsession arises from an intense sympathy for his brother, he shows us also the glory of feeling overleaping the restraints of the literal and the rational.

Sterne carries the duality of man to its ultimate expression. He comically exaggerates the outside view of man as a physically determined creature, the sport of chance or mechanical causation, the lonely product of a valueless material world. He exaggerates no less the inside view of man as a creature of feeling, convinced phenomenologically that he has a soul, creating the world in which he chiefly lives by the energy of his own imagination. The disjunction is as violent as Pascal's. Each man exists at once in what Thomas Browne called "divided and distinguished worlds." Nor does he find the reconciliations the Augustans sought in an order of mind supple enough to participate in orders above and below and firm enough to hold them together in harmony. Sterne envisages such a balance, as his sermons make clear, but in his fiction he exploits the imbalance, the fluctuation, the crazy veering between "delicacy" and "concupiscence." The Augustans always make the balance an indefinable and elusive point. It is stated by negations, caught in the delicate poise between the excesses of statement, protected by strategic retreat from every attempt to fix it in formula. We see it as the fulcrum of a thousand different antitheses, in the tone of a voice engaged in dialectical play, or the ironic self-corrections of stance. For all the challenges of Fielding's narrator, we feel that he personifies this balance. We are never allowed this much security in Sterne. The central order of mind drops out of view (although it can still be felt in the play of intelligence and comic detachment), and we are left with radical alternations of derision and sentiment.

Love for Sterne, as for Fielding, is the clearest instance of duality. Walter Shandy cites the two Venuses of Plato and his Renaissance commentators: "The first, which is the golden chain let down from heaven, excites to love heroic, which comprehends in it, and excites to the desire of philosophy and truth—the second, excites to *desire*, simply" (8,33). We see the puzzles in Toby's questions whether he is simply irritated by a blister in his "nethermost part" or in love with the Widow Wadman—"till the blister breaking in the one case——and the other remaining——my uncle Toby was presently convinced, that his wound was not a skin-deep-wound——but that it had gone to his heart" (8, 26). We see them in the Beguine's tender treatment of Trim. She rubs his wounded leg, "till at length, by two or three strokes longer than the rest——my passion rose to the highest pitch——I seiz'd her hand——" This conversion of irritation to passion, Tristram concludes, "contain'd in it the essence of all the love-romances which ever have been wrote since the beginning of the world" (8, 22). We see the incongruity most sharply in Slawkenbergius's tale, where the doleful courtly lover rides sighing through Strasburg, obliviously exhibiting his astonishingly large and obscene nose. He remains sublimely engaged in his tender and exalted sentiment, while the spectacle of his nose titallates the mass of Strasburgers to a carnival of erotic frenzy and the graver ones to the heat of scholastic dispute.

Sterne is equally willing to trace the highest and most stately activities down to the erotic energy they sublimate, and to overturn the stateliest structures so that their precariousness becomes clear. The large-nosed stranger alternately addresses his beloved mistress (up there and far away) and his refractory mule (down here and close): "O Julia, my lovely Julia!—nay I cannot stop to let thee bite that thistle—that ever the suspected tongue of a rival should have robbed me of enjoyment when I was upon the point of tasting it" (4, opening section). Or we have the termination of Julia's tender farewell: " 'Tis a bitter draught, Diego, but oh! 'tis embitter'd still more by dying un——." Slawkenbergius, the scholarly editor, "supposes the word intended was *unconvinced*, but her strength would not enable her to finish her letter." The pathos of the unfinished letter descends nicely into sexual innuendo, just as when Diego writes his ode in charcoal, we are told that "he eased his mind against the wall." Sterne keeps alive the Augustan irony about "poetical evacuation." He is as much aware of the convertibility of terms as the conversion of sentiments; whatever goes up can also come down.

We can see Sterne's distrust of systems and forms again in his mockery of scholastic debates about baptism. At what point does the embryo become a person? If the child can be baptized in the womb with an injection-pipe, why can't we extend this marginal area and simply baptize the spermatozoa all at once, "after the ceremony of marriage, and before that of consummation?" (1, 20). Sterne constantly satirizes our tendency to take our mental abstractions for real entities, a tendency deeply built into all of our systems for achieving moral or legal consistency. The danger is that we become reluctant to sacrifice a system to the suppleness or novelty of experience. We become attached to our words and preserve them at any cost. When Walter cannot make sense of a text, he "decides to study the mystic and the allegoric sense, — here is some room to turn a man's self in" (3, 37). It is an amiable crotchet in Walter and a good instance of the way in which men turn the search for meaning into the delights of conundrum. But Sterne wishes us, I think, to remember as well such results as the exertions of the three brothers in Swift's *Tale of a Tub* on their father's testament, when words become forms behind which interest can hide. The mild obsessions of Walter and Toby are innocent comic versions of something much worse in designing men, who welcome the opacity of forms. Sterne's central characters are transparent men, in whom the soul stands naked, so that one can trace "all her maggots from their first engendering to their crawling forth" (1, 23).

Sterne does all he can to subvert words and forms. He plays upon the unexpected implications of words and makes a casual analogy go round and round on all fours. He topples the jargon of courtly love or stoical pride. He mocks the delicacy of nuns who split an obscene word into syllables, each taking half, in order to get it said to a stubborn mule. (One may recall that Swift's three brothers, when they cannot twist words to their will, break them into syllables, which prove more malleable.) He infects words with obscene suggestions, which, once released, spread like a plague and corrupt every simple reference to noses, whiskers, or crevices. He exploits typography, as he reproduces the form of a contract, in order to make clear (as Pope does with legal abbreviations) how much the authority of the law depends upon formality or mystery. And all this is related to the self-consciousness that is constantly subverting the larger forms of the book itself—insisting upon it as a printed thing, exploiting the arbitrariness of chapter divisions, calling attention to the artifice of fictional time or to the process of reading itself or, most of all, to the author's exercise of control. Readers of fiction are generally eager to surrender themselves to belief; so long as a novel is conducted with sufficient skill, its conventions are rapidly accepted. Sterne insists upon making us conscious of all we have commonly taken for granted. By pretending incompetence or indecision, by teasing us with false leads or cheating our logical expectations, he exposes the forms at every point. Fielding's subversion of his artistic form is his ultimate commentary on the moral life he is treating. Sterne's is that and something more; his book is more generally philosophical than Fielding's. Sterne moves from the problems of ethics into the general theory of knowledge; his satire is moral, but his comedy is epistemological.

The Subversion of Satire

Ronald Paulson

The oddness of Dr. Slop in the world of *Tristram Shandy* has often been noticed. He is the only caricature; his physical description, the muddy fall he takes before the reader first sees him, and his boorish behavior are all from the world of Smollett and the picaresque writers. Slop makes one suddenly aware of how different this world is in which the attack is ambiguous, reproof is mixed with love, and evil has become good. But each of the other characters carries a Dr. Slop within him, as well as Slop's contrary.

Walter, Toby, Yorick, and the rest are, of course, humor-characters, for whom humor means an amusing and endearing oddity; they are the amiable humorists of whom Stuart Tave writes. In a general sense public assumptions have changed, the Tory being replaced by the Whig. Sterne is a writer who is still aware of the Tory assumptions, however. Immensely pleased to be told by the old Earl of Bathurst that he was the successor of Swift and Pope, he makes us see his characters and situations first as the old satiric ones and then as the new recipients of comic-sympathetic laughter. The thesis is as much a part of the effect as the antithesis, and the transition becomes for Sterne a basic theme.

Tristram Shandy is constructed like a satire rather than a novel and presents within the first volume all the elements of the Tory fiction as composed by Swift. The plot is, as with Swift, the book itself, and the form closely resembles Swift's epitome (in *A Tale of a Tub*) of the seventeenth-century literature that can be called wit-writing or writing-as-process and the hack-writing that derived from it. These forms of expression disdained all tradition, authori-

From *Satire and the Novel in Eighteenth-Century England.* © 1967 by Yale University. Yale University Press, 1967.

ty, or rules, and their only virtue was the reflection of the writer's own eccentric mind. In both cases the object ridiculed is the same self-sufficiency of mind, except that by Sterne's time it had taken the form of the Richardsonian novel.

Sterne apparently saw the same difficulty as Fielding in *Pamela* and *Clarissa* — a discrepancy between the moral structure of the novel and the psychological reality portrayed. It is this discrepancy that Swift had brilliantly dramatized and exploited in the *Tale* and his other first-person satires, making the discrepancy convey a meaning of his own. His strategy was to put the story in a single first-person speaker who was allowed to follow the wanderings of his random thoughts rather than chronology or the careful juxtapositions manipulated by the Fielding narrator; he used realism as an appearance that concealed the satirist's imposed order, thus to a startling degree maintaining realism while, through the natural juxtaposition of ideas in a rambling discourse, conveying his own commentary on the apparent chaos presented. Sterne follows the same procedure, but with a story instead of a discourse (though he is often close to discourse) and with a more thoroughly realized speaker. Thus the same ironic or informative juxtapositions that in a Fielding novel always run the risk of appearing contrived are in *Tristram Shandy* perfectly explicable as the accidental association of ideas of a wandering mind. Tristram explains the method in his madness (something Swift's consistency would not allow his speaker to do):

> I was just going, for example, to have given you the great outlines of my uncle *Toby's* most whimsical character; — when my aunt *Dinah* and the coachman came a-cross us, and led us a vagary some millions of miles into the very heart of the planetary system: Notwithstanding all this you perceive that the drawing of my uncle *Toby's* character went on gently all the time. . . .
>
> By this contrivance the machinery of my work is of a species by itself; two contrary motions are introduced into it, and reconciled, which were thought to be at variance with each other. In a word, my work is digressive, and it is progressive too, — and at the same time.

In the first volume four subjects, or events, are covered that have no temporal or narrative connection whatever but are associated in Tristram's mind — Tristram's conception, Yorick's life and death, Walter's theories, and the character of Uncle Toby. Each, showing the wounding or maiming (even destroying) of a person, is closely connected thematically to the others. Thus as the *Tale of a Tub* pretends to be a piece of egregious hack-writing, so

Tristram Shandy pretends to be the autobiography of Tristram; actually, being devoted largely to the period before and immediately after his birth, it is about his father and uncle and the relation of the freewheeling mind to reality. It pretends to be a novel to end all novels, but it is actually a satire on novels and all examples of the unbridled mind.

Before qualifying this statement (as every generalization concerning *Tristram Shandy* has to be qualified), one should look at a specific example of the unbridled, traditionless mind in the narrator, Tristram. As Swift's Grub Street Hack or Richardson's Pamela repeatedly says, "I am now writing" (or "this very moment" or "this present month of August, 1697"), so Tristram speaks of a memorandum "which now lies upon the table" or refers to "this very day, in which I am now writing this book for the edification of the world [cf. the Hack's "for the universal benefit of mankind"], — which is March 9, 1759" or says "that observation is my own; — and was struck out by me [cf. "strike all Things out of themselves"] this very rainy day, *March 26, 1759*, and betwixt the hours of nine and ten in the morning." Most of all, there is Tristram's laborious attempt to establish the exact moment and circumstances of his own birth. Both Swift and Sterne are satirizing the importance of the present moment in the traditionless, unstable modern world. This moment is all the modern has to hold to because he has only himself; and so he makes it a rallying cry of defiance.

Like Swift, Sterne satirizes the author-reader relationship that such a notion implies. As the Grub Street Hack tells the reader exactly how he must read his book, even down to taking purges and living in a garret, so Tristram peremptorily orders his reader to "immediately turn back, that is, as soon as you get to the next full stop, and read the whole chapter over again" or "Lay down the book, and I will allow you half a day to give a probable guess at the grounds of this procedure." Tristram echoes the Hack's claim of "an absolute authority in right, as the freshest modern, which gives me a despotic power over all authors before me" in his refusal to follow any tradition, any authority. He at once dissociates his work from the precept of Horace (do not begin ab ovo), "for in writing that I have set about, I shall confine myself neither to his rules, nor to any man's rules that ever lived."

Sterne begins then with the Swiftean villain and his characteristic expression. He ignores the Fielding villain (unless Dr. Slop qualifies) who hides his natural impulses under masks that conform with the dictates of accepted social standards. His protagonist, like Swift's, tries to eliminate or deny discrepancy rather than conceal it and so attempts to shape reality to accord with his own image of what it should be. The hypocrite is a conformist; the world-changer, a nonconformist.

But although the Tristram who is narrator is a world-changer, the Tristram of the narrative is a passive and wholly innocent victim; if anyone could be more innocent than the young Joseph Andrews it is the newborn babe Tristram. The narrative is constructed around a series of satiric scenes of frustration, violence, and pain, either involving Tristram or contributing to one of his disasters—his begetting, Dr. Slop and the knots (and his excommunication of them), the crushing of Tristram's nose, the bungled christening, Phutatorius and the chestnut, the death of brother Bobby, the drastic circumcision, and so on. Approached from the direction of satire, the story Tristram tells is one great anatomy of the fools and knaves who affect him. His recollections are a long list of consequences to himself. Walter Shandy is more obviously than Tristram the satanic villain who tries to reorder the world because of the effects of his work and his defeats at the hands of reality. Another kind of world-changer, he "was systematical, and, like all systematical reasoners, he would move both heaven and earth, and twist and torture everything in nature to support his hypothesis." "What is the character of a family to an hypothesis?" he asks. This man, "a philosopher in grain,—speculative,—systematical," is of course a descendant of Swift's crazy and dangerous speculators in religion, learning, and science. The Grub Street Hack, in order to arrive at his particular interpretation of reality, intended to "lay open, by untwisting or unwinding, and either to draw up by exantlation, or display by incision." One after another, Walter's hypotheses, like the Hack's, are proved wrong when they come face to face with reality. In every case, however, defeat is accompanied by the consequence to young Tristram.

For the idea of the pedantic father, the lover of hypotheses who plans his child's birth, christening, and education all according to some fantastic theories derived from the ancients, Sterne drew in particular upon *The Memoirs of Martinus Scriblerus*. This product of the Scriblerus Club offered a prototype for Walter and even a general model for Sterne's plot. The emergence of Tristram as a participating character in volume 7 is not unlike young Martin's emergence toward the end of the Scriblerian fragment. In both cases the emphasis is clearly on the father up to this point. Indeed perhaps because the Scriblerian project petered out and thus less was written on Martin, Sterne was initially led to put his emphasis predominantly on Walter.

Cornelius Scriblerus begins to plan for his child before conception, believing that the state of the homunculus is crucially important. He follows the prescription of Galen, "confining himself and his wife for almost the whole first year to Goat's Milk and Honey"; he will have sexual intercourse with his wife only when the wind is right; and once Martin is conceived, he has a concert performed every day ("according to the custom of the Magi"). Long before it is time for Martin's birth he prepares "two Treatises of Education; the one he called, *A Daughter's Mirrour*, and the other *A Son's Monitor*." All of these theories are based on his love of the ancients — on precedent, custom, old books, everything except common sense and experience.

It is Cornelius's wife and young Martin who suffer for his theories. He causes his wife to undergo an abortion and is very pleased when he learns the aborted child was female. He nearly kills Martin when he attempts to christen him according to old custom. His idea is to have Martin christened on an ancient, rusty shield, but a conscientious maid polishes off the rust, and at the sight "Cornelius sunk back on a chair, the guests stood astonished, the infant squal'd." He drops both shield and child to the floor, and his only concern is whether the former has been damaged.

Walter's theories parallel Cornelius's, down to his theory of the homunculus, his once-a-month intercourse, and his *Tristrapoedia*. In the same way, it is Tristram and his mother who suffer as a result of Walter's pedantic interpretation of the marriage contract and his choice of a male midwife who wrote a book on the subject instead of an experienced midwife. Martin's christening is the single episode in the *Memoirs* that may have suggested to Sterne all the various disasters that befall Tristram and Walter's plans for him. Walter's own suffering, though hardly minimal, is, like Cornelius's, directed at his ruined theory rather than the ruined child. When news reaches him of the forceps accident or the false christening, he flings himself down on a bed or whatever is handy, but he never does the first natural thing — run up to see his wife or son. He worries about the body politic, which he describes in vivid concreteness, but not about the bodies of his wife and child.

Walter's overreliance on mind at the expense of body is the cause of his error. Like all the satanic villains of the Augustans, he is in various senses impotent. There is a Shandy tradition of sexual failure, but it is essentially Walter's emotional impotence that prevents him from feeling any sexual passion. He begets children "out of principle," and his conception of Tristram, which I earlier compared to Achitophel's conception of his "lump of anarchy," has nothing to do with passion. His desire is to mold the unborn Tristram into an abstract pattern of his own formulation.

His first defeat is appropriately at the hands of his wife, who endangers Tristram's homunculus by asking about the clock at the wrong moment. But if, like Jonathan Wild and others, he is thwarted by the opposite sex, he is also drubbed by the world as a whole. Swift uses the hard realities of objects like forceps and sash weights to suggest the immutable order of the universe which a speculative mind like Walter's cannot alter to his own ends.

Sterne follows this equation closely, creating all the typical scenes of reality collapsing theory, but he emphasizes the irrationality of the real world, not its order or even ideality. For example, after explaining how, as a result of his elaborate theories of naming, Walter hates the name Tristram, Tristram writes:

> When this story is compared with the title page, — Will not the gentle reader pity my father from his soul? — to see an orderly and well-disposed gentleman, who tho' singular, — yet inoffensive in his notions, — so played upon in them by cross purposes; — to look down upon the stage, and see him baffled and overthrown in all his little systems and wishes; to behold a train of events perpetually falling out against him, and in so critical and cruel a way, as if they had purposedly been plann'd and pointed against him, merely to insult his speculations. — In a word, to behold such a one, in his old age, ill-fitted for troubles, ten times in a day suffering sorrow; — ten times in a day calling the child of his prayers Tristram! . . . By his ashes! I swear it, — if ever malignant spirit took pleasure, or busied itself in traversing the purposes of mortal man, — it must have been here.

By playing with the time sequence, Tristram shows Walter as old and worn, a tiny human on the great impersonal stage of the world, and suggests a lack of connection between men's minds and the objective world under any circumstances.

It is suggestive that the Swiftean villain Walter Shandy was chosen by *The London Magazine* of 1782 as one of its two favorite comic "humourists." He came to represent the Shandean philosopher or system-builder, whose soaring imagination was comically contrasted with its petty defeats at the hands of reality—a Quixote, in short. It is equally significant that the second of these favorite "humourists" was Matthew Bramble, the satirist transformed into a comic type. The two types that are polarized in Bramble and Walter Shandy and continue in novels of the nineteenth century were neatly distinguished by Congreve:

> a Character of a Splenetick and Peevish *Humour* should have a Satyrical Wit. A Jolly and Sanguine *Humour* should have a Facetious Wit. The Former should speak Positively; the Latter, Carelessly: For the former Observes and shews things as they are; the latter rather overlooks Nature, and speaks things as he would have them.

Here is the basic attitude of the fictionalist toward satire near the end of the century. Satire is a necessary means to observe and show "things as they are," but it is an excess in itself and thus can appear in only one way in the novel—divided between the satirist and his satiric object, in a splenetic character who will keep the characters in line and a ridiculous character who is his foil.

A comic character is, however, by no means the end of Sterne's effect in *Tristram Shandy*. He accomplishes the undermining of Walter to a large extent by making Tristram, the writer-to-the-moment, a foil to Walter's straightjacketed mind. Both Tristram the child (as victim) and Tristram the man (as liberated mind) act as the reality with which Walter's theories come into constant conflict; they, along with Uncle Toby's nonsensical common sense, represent the real world. In a sense Sterne interprets *A Tale of a Tub* as many of Swift's contemporaries did, as simply advocating the chaos of experiential reality. He does with the image of chaos almost the reverse of what Swift did, restoring the positive value it had for Rabelais and Erasmus. The irregular and vital are even connected with Hogarth's "Line of Beauty," the natural curving line opposed to the geometrical symmetry of Palladian architecture and neoclassicism. Corporal Trim, when he begins to read the essay on conscience, is presented first in a hypothetical military posture, "dividing the weight of his body equally upon both legs; — his eye fix'd, as if on duty," and then in his actual stance, with his knee, for example, "bent, but that not violently, — but so as to fall within the limits of the line of beauty; — and I add, of the line of science too," for otherwise all orators "must fall upon their noses."

This is not, however, the complete effect. In *The Memoirs of Scriblerus* the plot was split between Cornelius and Martin, father and son, who were made to represent the two extremes of eccentricity—the mad ancient and the equally mad modern. While Cornelius reduced everything to the narrowest interpretation of the ancients' precedents, Martin went out hither and yon to collect scientific specimens and seek a "modern" education. In Scriblerian satire the unbridled and too bridled mind are two extremes of the same evil, and Sterne retains this implication by suggesting that Walter and Tristram are equally mad. Finally, they tend to represent two kinds of experience, two ways of ordering that are opposed and left to comment *on each other* and are comic in juxtaposition.

Much the same applies to the rest of the dramatis personae of Augustan satire as they appear in *Tristram Shandy*. Yorick is the satirist who is isolated from "decent" society by his propensity for seeing and telling the truth and subsequently is driven to his grave. The other character, Uncle Toby, is both a commonsenisical foil to Walter (an ingénu satirist) and in his own right a modern who tries to impose his version of reality (here the battle of Namur) on his contemporaries just as Walter tries to impose his theories; he is always explaining, explaining, and is never understood. Even Yorick, to his contemporaries, is a madman who cannot be understood. Thus, although Walter is shown to be completely isolated and alone, like the Grub Street Hack or the astrologer Partridge, so are his victim and the satirist and the whole cast. Moreover, the impotence of the satanic villain, both as to his deeds and his sexual prowess, while evident enough in Walter, is famous in Toby and Tristram and, in a somewhat different sense, in Yorick. Walter's world-changing theories are defeated, but so in various ways are the plans of all the other characters. All of them are presented as not only contrasting but parallel cases. From the idea of the thwarted hypothesizer Sterne develops the suffering figure of Walter and the equally suffering figure of Tristram: they have become real people, not symbols. From the argument between Cornelius and his brother (or brother-in-law) Albertus comes the wonderful conversations between Walter and Toby. These also doubtless owe something to Quixote's talks with Sancho Panza. As usual in the eighteenth-century novel, Don Quixote is the extra ingredient added to the formula of the Scriblerus memoirs. Cornelius becomes Don Quixote and thus lovable; Albertus becomes Sancho. Sterne's curious wildness of tone, which makes the whole matter of satire somewhat questionable, comes from the quixotic nature of the follies examined. As Quixote went out to save maidens in distress, so Toby relives the war of the Spanish Succession, Walter weaves his elaborate theories, and Tristram tries to write his life "to the moment." Both Walter and Toby go wrong by reading the books in their ancestral library — Walter, the works of the logicians and the philosophers, the makers of minute and elaborate hypotheses; Toby, the romances of war and adventure, *Guy of Warwick* and *The Seven Champions of Christendom*.

One is reminded of Sterne's earliest published work, *A Good Warm Watch-Coat, or The Political Romance* (1759), in which he presents a very Swiftean allegory, reminiscent of the story of the brothers and their coats in the *Tale*, with various letters and the like tacked on (at the end in this case) to set the allegory in perspective. His workmanship is skillful but conventional, with a touch of life here and there, but in the "key" that is appended to the "romance," he reveals his more characteristic manner. This second fiction has a club that reads and discusses the allegory, more reminiscent of the old *Post Boy* satire showing a club reading and commenting on the mail than of the Spectator Club. While the allegory is a fair imitation of Swift, the round-table discussion is pure Sterne. It abandons the conventional playing off of true and false views and instead introduces the interplay of different and incompatible points of view that are mutually personal and obtuse, much as Smollett does a decade later in *Humphry Clinker*.

Swift's *Tale* attacked the impossibility of communication — the intellectual impotence that results from pride in one's own mental gyrations. When Sterne's second volume specifically extends the theme of sexual impotence to a less elemental equivalent, communication, one can see that the book has been, from the start, about this problem. It is about hobbyhorses—Toby's, Walter's, and, by implication, Tristram's. In volume one hobbyhorses characterize the man; in volume two the various hobbyhorses or streams of associations of ideas collide. Toby's crosses Walter's, Dr. Slop's crosses these, and so on.

Toby's hobbyhorse, with which the volume begins, is the outcome of an attempt to communicate; he has to make himself understood as to exactly how and where he was wounded, and so he ends by building Namur in his bowling green. At the beginning of the volume, he offers a close parallel to Tristram's hobbyhorse: both are searches into the past to determine and communicate the exact nature and causes of their woundings. Toby traces trajectories and plots exact coordinates of his position at the crucial moment, and this leads him to other woundings, other battles, and even whole wars. Tristram begins the same way and branches out to other "small heroes" who, like himself, are crushed by the world—the LeFevers, Marias, Tobys, Yoricks, and Walters. The account of Toby's fortifications (the growth of his hobbyhorse) in volume 2 is a concrete illustration of Tristram's own adjustment to life: in volume 1 Tristram indicates the sort of buffets life has given him and suggests an analogue in Toby; then in volume 2 he shows how Toby adjusts to his situation via a hobbyhorse. By the constant asides to the reader it becomes obvious that Toby's solution tells why Tristram himself is writing. The only way to survive in such a world is to have a hobbyhorse.

Speaking of Toby's futile attempts to convey his meaning, Tristram says, " 'Twas not by ideas,—by heaven! his life was put in jeopardy by words." It is, of course, words that cause the collision of hobbyhorses. Curtins and hornworks, which are seige equipment to Toby, are bed curtains and cuckold horns to the lecherous Dr. Slop. Words come to mean outer forms that conceal reality; they come to have an utterly false and arbitrary meaning that is beyond an individual's control. To dramatize this, Sterne introduces a series of conventional documents in the first two volumes—in volume 1, the marriage contract and the opinion of the doctors of the Sorbonne; in volume 2, the Sermon on Conscience. The first two are examples of attempts to rationalize and legalize, to write the letter of the law, on important subjects that will not allow it (a husband-wife relationship and the nature of a human being). "I was doom'd," says Tristram, "by marriage articles, to have my nose squeez'd as flat to my face, as if the destinies had actually spun me without one." The Sermon on Conscience comes as a further caveat against overreliance on external forms of control and also against conscience itself when it is self-deluded and sets up for king.

Against these ordered documents, Sterne places the shiftiness of the potential meanings of words. He turns again to Swift's *Tale*, where the Grub Street Hack's failure to order reality according to his own eccentric vision appears most strikingly in his failure to control the meaning of words. The tub to which he compares his writing becomes, in a slightly different context, the literal tub in which dissenters preached or in which syphilitics were sweated. Once tub has established the idea of a container, it moves to analogous shapes (the rotten nut, the sack posset), always with the modern's equation between any product of his brain and the modern himself (they are, Swift maintains, the same). These images reach a climax in the concrete figure of the Aeolist who makes his body a mere container of air (spirit), and the spider (in the *Battle of the Books*) whose body is a self-sufficient tub of dirt out of which he constructs his cobwebs.

Thus Tristram, who has been talking about his birth, refers to the joke Yorick makes on one of his pompous parishioners in terms of gestation: the effect of the joke grows in the victim (though forgotten by Yorick) until finally, when the opportunity shows itself, out comes a full-grown revenge. The result, Yorick's loss of preferment, leads to a general disillusionment with mankind that kills Yorick; he tells Eugenius as he is dying to look at his head, "so bruised and misshapen'd with the blows which ***** and *****, and some others have so unhandsomely given me in the dark." This image is picked up in volume 2 when Dr. Slop knocks at the Shandy door, which "crushed the head of as notable and curious a dissertation as ever was engendered in the womb of speculation; — it was some months before my father could get an opportunity to be safely deliver'd of it"; later one sees the result of Dr. Slop's forceps on Tristram's head.

Words never mean the same thing to one person as to another, to Walter as to Toby, or to Tristram as to the reader; each goes his separate way, contributing to the general meaning of the novel. In *Tristram Shandy* words are part of man's original dislocation. They are like Walter's theories, analogous to the clocks that are not wound, the hinges that do not get oiled, the sash weights that are not replaced, the fields that are never cultivated, and the coats of arms that are never repaired. Appropriately, words keep slipping into their sexual meanings, and verbal misunderstandings lead to the malfunctioning of objects which, in turn, leads to the literal or figurative emasculations of the characters. Sterne implies that the difficulty in communication is caused by the external forms of the words themselves or at least by man's inability or unwillingness to use them correctly. Tristram is accordingly compelled, in order to convey his meaning, to adopt the most unorthodox methods, which include introducing marbled pages, violating chronology, and introducing a dedication out of place. Even the "digressive . . . progressive" mode of his work is no longer a satiric strategy as much as a proper means of communicating a nonrational meaning. The puns on gestation and crushed heads, for example, suggest the analogy between Yorick and Tristram and (whether by Tristram or Sterne) connect all these battered people—the unborn Tristram, his father whose disillusionment is to come with Tristram, Toby already twenty years older than his wound, and Yorick who dies years later when Tristram is a grown man. The multimeanings of words help to focus these four crucial incidents, scattered in time, on Tristram's birth.

On the level of the characters, Toby has to show the location of his wounding by maps and models and (for the Widow Wadman) in the flesh; Trim's stance as a "Line of Beauty" and later his dropping his hat to convey the death of Bobby are more important than spoken words with strict denotation. Walter is constantly flying into rages when Toby applies common sense to his theories or gets astride his own hobbyhorse, but by gesture or some other nonrational means, Toby does communicate his love to Walter. "My uncle Toby stole his hand unperceived behind his chair, to give my father's hand a squeeze——." When Toby, angry at Walter's ridicule of his hobbyhorse, puffs so hard on his pipe that Walter begins to cough, he at once leaps up in sympathy, despite his painful groin. Toby's actions, in turn, "cut my father thro' his reins, for the pain he had just been giving him." On the other hand, a strain of *Lillibullero* or a look from Toby can transform Walter, and they communicate sensitively through "hems," short broken sentences, and dashes simulating silence. Even Dr. Slop can be communicated with by a "humph," and the Widow Wadman and Mrs. Shandy talk with their eyes. In volume 3 these modes of communication are illustrated in the stories of the Abbess of Andouillet and the ass and of Tristram and the ass in the doorway. Words do not suffice to move the ass; neither does food; but a good blow from behind does. The nonrational that rises above these is the reality Sterne is trying to represent, and so communication is achieved by gesture, irrational sounds, and often complete silence. At this point Sterne is consciously connecting Tristram with those Augustan fools who, like the Grub Street Hack, convey their meaning through eccentricities of form, italics, and whatnot. Walter and Toby are the enthusiasts who communicate through coughs and belches. Sterne has taken the step from Swift's world to Wordsworth's. As Toby and Walter cannot understand each others' words, so Wordsworth is unable to understand the words of the solitary reaper. But there is a higher kind of communication—by love or feeling—that takes place naturally between Toby and Walter when all else has failed. Addison, Pope, and Fielding continue Swift's attack on the senseless sounds of the Italian opera singer and the hack poet, but Sterne sees this pure sound as the final reality and truth.

Fielding demonstrates in his novels a movement in this direction. In *Tom Jones* the "gentle pressure" of the baby Tom's hand "seeming to implore his assistance" has more effect on Allworthy than "the eloquence of Mrs. Deborah" who wants to cast out the baby. But these examples of natural reactions opposed to formalized ones bear little relation to the extremities to which Sterne goes for his examples. He consciously takes up the old satiric object, lets one see that it is a satiric object, and then modifies it into a good. In his own terms he arrives at irrational communication not as an ideal but as a last feeble hope. It is not, after all, a very effective means of communicating: it does not prevent any of the physical catastrophes; it only signals the lowest common denominator—that we are all related in some sense. *Tristram Shandy* is not so much praise of the irrational modes of understanding (as Wordsworth's "Solitary Reaper" is) as an attack on the faulty rational ones and thus on the Swiftean assumption that there is an alternative to the enthusiast's exalted coughs and hems.

In the same way Sterne shows that the particular moment—"this very rainy day, *March* 26, 1759, and betwixt the hours of nine and ten in the morning"—is transient and insignificant, but he also suffuses it with irrational importance. His particular effect is, as I have said, the romantic irony of complicating the reader's reaction through satire followed by acceptance. It must also be concluded that, in relation to our general study of the novel, he has picked up one strand of the antiromance tradition and written the ultimate expression of a-literature in the eighteenth century. He accomplishes this feat by subverting the conventions not only of Richardson but of Swift and Fielding as well.

The Comic Syntax
of *Tristram Shandy*

Ian Watt

Laurence Sterne received no notice in the annual bibliography of the *Philological Quarterly* for 1953. Since then there has been a rapid increase in published studies, but there are, as yet, few signs of converging perspectives in our view of *Tristram Shandy*. There are, of course, many things that recent studies have enabled us to see more clearly—its philosophical and literary traditions, the details of sources or of characterization; but these approaches hardly resolve the elementary problems which the reader faces as he tries to come to grips with the text. One of these problems, which persists even after many readings, concerns the unity of *Tristram Shandy*. A good deal has been done to demonstrate unity of plot and character, using the criteria that are traditional in dealing with the novel; what follows explores a very different, though not necessary contradictory, approach to the problem.

We can probably recognize a passage taken at random from *Tristram Shandy* more quickly than one from any other book. The tone, the style, the attitude toward the reader, and the events, all are quite special; and they don't vary substantially from page to page or from beginning to end. One thing that is consistent in *Tristram Shandy* is its narrative voice.

Consider, for example, the opening paragraph:

> I wish either my father or my mother, or indeed both of them,
> as they were in duty both equally bound to it, had minded what
> they were about when they begot me; had they duly considered
> how much depended upon what they were then doing;——that

From *Studies in Criticism and Aesthetics 1660–1800*, edited by Howard Anderson and John S. Shea. © 1967 by the University of Minnesota. University of Minnesota Press, 1967.

not only the production of a rational Being was concerned in it, but that possibly the happy formation, and temperature of his body, perhaps his genius and the very cast of his mind; — and, for aught they knew to the contrary, even the fortunes of his whole house might take their turn from the humours and dispositions which were then uppermost; — Had they duly weighed and considered all this, and proceeded accordingly, — I am verily persuaded I should have made a quite different figure in the world, from that in which the reader is likely to see me. (1, 1)

Taking notice of the promise of the title, we see that in a sense we are getting what we expect in this first chapter — the hero's begetting. It is whimsically done, to be sure, if only because we are unaccustomed to thinking about this particular action from the point of view of the end product; but after all, we may reflect, the author is only taking the conventions of autobiographical fiction with unprecedented literalness, and, with a vengeance, beginning at the beginning. Such a view of the text, which would still see it primarily as a novel, would continue to find some support from the ostensive narrative subject of the next six books; they proceed from Tristram's conception to his parturition, baptism, and breeching. But, of course, Sterne's main interest doesn't really lie with the traumatic consequences of these no doubt important events in his hero's life, as we can see from the way that none of them plays any part later except as a topic of jest, and, more important, that virtually nothing else about Tristram's life emerges.

At this point, if not before, we must take account of Sterne's epigraph, from Epictetus: "It is not things themselves that disturb men, but their judgments about these things." What matters, Sterne is telling us, is not particular actions, but the reflective consideration of them in the judging mind. In the passage quoted, for instance, even the grammar makes the action subordinate to reflection about it: we have to get through the first two lines — "I wish either my father or my mother, or indeed both of them, as they were in duty both equally bound to it, had minded what they were about" before we know the cause of the speaker's impatience; and when it is specified it comes in a subordinate clause: "when they begot me."

There is a further departure from the usual fictional emphasis on narrative event when Tristram proceeds:

— Believe me, good folks, this is not so inconsiderable a thing as many of you may think it; — you have all, I dare say, heard of the animal spirits, as how they are transfused from father to

son, etc. etc. —— and a great deal to that purpose: —— Well, you
may take my word, that nine parts in ten of a man's sense or
his nonsense, his successes and miscarriages in this world depend
upon their motions and activity, and the different tracts and trains
you put them into, so that when they are once set a-going, whether
right or wrong, 'tis not a halfpenny matter, —— away they go cluttering like hey-go mad; and by treading the same steps over and
over again, they presently make a road of it, as plain and as smooth
as a garden-walk, which, when they are once used to, the Devil
himself sometimes shall not be able to drive them off it. (1, 1)

Here Tristram seems to be thinking less of the event than of his auditors
as he anticipates their derisive incredulity that, even after some forty years,
he should still be so disgruntled at the thought of parental irresponsibility.
"Believe me, good folks, this is not so inconsiderable a thing as many of
you may think it; —— you have all, I dare say, heard of the animal spirits."
"And if you haven't, you peasants, cringe," implies Tristram's lofty "I dare
say"; and the paragraph continues to focus our attention so completely on
Tristram's present claim on our commiseration and on the dangers of not
granting it that we have almost forgotten Mr. and Mrs. Shandy.

They reappear for the final brief paragraph of the first chapter, but in
a way that continues their subordination to Tristram's directing mind in at
least three respects:

Pray, my Dear, quoth my mother, *have you not forgot to wind up
the clock? Good* G——! cried my father, making an exclamation,
but taking care to moderate his voice at the same time, —— *Did
ever woman, since the creation of the world, interrupt a man with such
a silly question?* Pray, what was your father saying? —— Nothing.
(1, 1)

Again, the narrative event is merely an occasion for talking. This time,
however, the talk isn't soliloquy but conversation: first, conversation between
the characters; and second, between the narrator and his audience. It's out
of the combination of these two elements that the humor and suspense of
the chapter arise; and these in turn ultimately depend upon Tristram's presence,
more specifically on his withholding from his audience the narrative information required to understand the scene until it is needed for his comic climax:
obviously all the connubial converse about the clock, and Tristram's reflections about it, remain fairly obscure until the reader's oscillation between

bewilderment and understanding is finally resolved through Tristram's answer to the question interposed by his imaginary reader. " 'Pray, what was your father saying?' " — " 'Nothing.' "

The design of the first chapter as a whole, then, reveals that Tristram's primary emphasis is rhetorical rather than narrative; we have to wait another three chapters before we fully understand Mrs. Shandy's question about winding the clock, but the chapter has perfect formal completeness in its own rhetorical terms, since the reader's questions in the first paragraph begin to be answered in the second, and are fully disposed of by the final clinching implication of the word "Nothing." Narrative as such is not autonomous or primary; it is merely the initial fictional pretext for a complex pattern of conversations: conversation between characters, in the first place; and, more important, conversation between Tristram and his readers. It is essentially the completion of this interplay, rather than that of a narrative episode, which determines Sterne's organization of his basic compositional unit, the chapter.

As we go on, indeed, it becomes apparent that the same rhetorical imperatives govern the interrelationship between chapters. Thus if we turn to the climax of the other main plot of *Tristram Shandy*, the courtship of Uncle Toby and the Widow Wadman in the last two books, we find exactly the same subordination of narrative development to the autonomous demands of rhetorical effect. In book 8, for example, when, at long last, the Widow Wadman trains upon Uncle Toby the full fire-power of her amorous eye, under the pretense that there's a speck of dirt in it which he must remove: "— I am half distracted, Captain *Shandy*, said Mrs. *Wadman*, holding up her cambric handkerchief to her left eye, as she approached the door of my Uncle *Toby's* sentry-box — a mote — or sand — or something — I know not what, has got into this eye of mine — do look into it — it is not in the white — " (8, 24).

Up to now this is straightforward comic narrative, but there follows a long commentary by Tristram, who concludes chapter 24 with the adjuration: "If thou lookest, uncle *Toby*, in search of this mote one moment longer — thou art undone."

In chapter 25, after Tristram's long military simile, "An eye is for all the world exactly like a cannon," has reminded us of the parallel between the wars of love and those of Uncle Toby, we are finally taken back to the fictional scene:

> I protest, Madam, said my uncle *Toby*, I can see nothing whatever in your eye.
>
> It is not in the white; said Mrs. *Wadman*: my uncle *Toby* looked with might and main into the pupil —

Once again the comedy of misunderstanding is interrupted by the narrator's bravura description of the eye's message, and the chapter ends when he finally interrupts himself with the reflection:

> But I shall be in love with it myself, if I say another word about it. — It did my uncle *Toby's* business.

That the interlocking of chapters is conceived primarily in rhetorical rather than fictional terms is clear enough: here a single narrative incident is related in two separate chapters, each with a parallel compositional structure, emphasized by the choric repetition of their closing phrase: "thou art un*done*"; and, "It *did* my uncle Toby's business."

The narrative event — Toby's falling in love — is a momentous one that has long been heralded; but Tristram does not use it for a full descriptive or psychological presentation of the event in its own right. Of the three main comic climaxes, for instance, only one, Mrs. Wadman's repetition of "It is not in the white," belongs within the fictional framework; the other two depend either on byplay with an imaginary reader — "it was not, Madam, a rolling eye" — or on Tristram's sudden transition from his own imaginary reaction to the widow's left eye to his confidential anticipation of poor Toby's doom: "It did my uncle Toby's business."

The structure of Sterne's larger compositional units, then, is based on the rhetorical patterns arising out of the complex tripartite pattern of conversation between the narrator, his fictional characters, and his auditors. Exactly the same can be said of the smaller compositional units, from the clause to the paragraph; *Tristram Shandy* has at least one kind of unity, unity of style; and behind the style there is, of course, the man and his view of life.

"Writing, when properly managed, (as you may be sure I think mine is) is but a different name for conversation," Tristram himself tells us. His prose reflects the brilliance and ease of a great age of conversation whose most splendid historical record is Boswell's *Life of Johnson*. Sterne's style retains some elements of the careful parallelism and balance of sound, syntax, and meaning that we think of as typical of the Augustans. In the opening sentence, for instance, there is the balanced pattern of consonantal stops, "b," "d," and "t," which gives a certain sense of order to the petulant impression of the sounds themselves: "I wish either *my father* or *my mother*, or in*deed* both of *them*, as *they* were in *duty* both equally bound to it, had min*ded* what they were a*bout* when they *bego*t me . . ." The symmetry, however, is largely concealed by the tone of conversational abandon, most evident in the colloquialism ("minded what they were about"); the reader at once feels that he is being directly addressed in an easy and unbuttoned way, and that the units of meaning are being strung together in the most spontaneous way.

The most obvious indication of this conversational style is the punctuation, and especially the use of the dash. In the short chapter about Widow Wadman's eye (8, 25), for example, there are more dashes—eighteen—than any other mark of punctuation; and even though the proportion is rarely as high elsewhere, there must be very few pages of *Tristram Shandy* which do not have many more dashes than is usual in any but the most amateurish writing.

The reasons for this great reliance on the dash go deep into the nature of Sterne's creative strategy. The dash is virtually proscribed in expository prose, presumably because it flouts the standard requirement that the verbal components of a sentence should be articulated into a coherent syntactical structure, a structure in which the subordination and superordination of all the parts should express the unity and direction of the sentence as a whole. Sterne's affront to conventional syntax is essential to establishing the qualities he required for Tristram's voice; Sterne didn't want unity or coherence or defined direction, at least in any conventional sense; he wanted multiplicity, not unity; he wanted free association of ideas, not subordination of them; he wanted to go backwards or forwards or sideways, not in straight linear paths.

We are, of course, quite used to these kinds of discontinuity in ordinary colloquial conversation. In the Widow Wadman's speech, for instance ("A mote—or sand—or something—I know not what, has got into this eye of mine—do look into it—it is not in the white") the dash is used as much to mark pauses as anything else; whatever meaning may be left obscure by the syntax is clarified by the implied situations and gestures; and it is the dashes which force the reader to imagine them. Elsewhere the dash is used merely for aggregating units, as in the dazzling series of descriptive phrases about the Widow Wadman's left eye; and here we observe the usefulness of the dash in Sterne's characteristic exploitation of the rhetorical expectations aroused by any extended verbal series. But the most important strategic function of the dash, both in these passages and in general, is to serve Tristram as a nonlogical junction between different kinds of discourse: between past and present; between narrative event and authorial address to the reader; between one train of thought and another in Tristram's mind.

Sterne needed a much looser and less directed junction between units of meaning than normal syntax allows, for his psychology, for his narrative mode, for his manipulation of the reader, and for expressing his view of life. Dashes were invaluable for enacting the drama of inhibited impulse, of the sudden interruptions and oscillations of thought and feeling, which characterize Tristram both as a person and as a narrator. One obvious example of the latter occurs when there is an abrupt and unheralded shift in the point of view of the narration. Consider, for example, in the chapter cited above, the passage where the narrator comments: "there never was an eye of them all, so fitted to rob my uncle *Toby* of his repose, as the very eye, at which he was looking — it was not, Madam, a rolling eye . . ." Here the dash enables Tristram to turn suddenly from Toby to reprove an imaginary female interlocutor for her licentious ocular deportment. Similarly the rhetorical finality of the close of the chapter depends upon the dash on which hinges Tristram's sudden temporal transition from his own present attitude toward the eye to its devastating effect, nearly two generations ago, on Captain Shandy: "It did my uncle Toby's business."

Tristram's prose style, then, embodies the multiplicity of his narrative point of view; it is idiosyncratic because it serves a unique, and often puzzling, combination of functions. One of these, at least, demands further attention here, since it is both important in itself, and closely related to some of the main differences of interpretation to which *Tristram Shandy* has given rise.

Tristram's voice, as we have seen, is uniquely adapted to rapid transitions, and they are an essential element in his humor. Kant wrote that "laughter arises from the sudden transformation of a strained expectation into nothing"; Sterne is a master at such transformations, undermining the expectation that has been built up by suddenly making Tristram change his point of view. The end of Le Fever's life, for example, offers a famous example: we are at the deathbed:

> The blood and spirits of *Le Fever*, which were waxing cold and slow within him, and were retreating to their last citadel, the heart — rallied back, — the film forsook his eyes for a moment, — he looked up wishfully in my uncle *Toby's* face, — then cast a look upon his boy, — and that *ligament*, fine as it was, — was never broken. —
>
> Nature instantly ebbed again, — the film returned to its place, — the pulse fluttered — stopped — went on — throbbed — stopped again — moved — stopped — shall I go on? — No. (6, 10)

Here, of course, the humor arises out of the abrupt transition from narration to a direct address to the reader, which suddenly relieves the reader just at the moment when his suffering from the pathos of Le Fever's death has become unendurable; and the relief is easily achieved because only a dash is needed to switch us from the world where fiction seems real (as is typical in the novel) to the world where Tristram can jog the reader's elbow to remind him that his fiction is, after all, only fiction.

Tristram's attitude to his audience is in part that of the ventriloquist and in part that of the jester. Where he is recounting the actions and dialogues of the Shandy household, multiple impersonation is called for; and Tristram is an expert in vocal mimicry as in the external description of the dialogues between his characters. It is interesting, in this connection, to note Sterne's admiration of the famous Parisian preacher Père Clement, who, he wrote, converted his pulpit into a stage, so that "the variety of his tones [made] you imagine there were no less than five or six actors on it together."

But the main dialogue which Tristram carries on is with the reader; at least half of *Tristram Shandy* is taken up not with narrative but with direct address to the audience by Tristram, often about matters only tangentially related to the story.

For this dialogue, the first need is for Tristram to ensure that his readers never lose themselves so completely in the story that they forget the monologist behind the footlights. One way of reminding the readers of his presence is for Tristram to break down the cold impersonality of print, whose impassive objectivity encourages us in most novels to forget the literary mirror in which the fictional world is reflected. The typographical tricks, the short or blank or misnumbered chapters, the squiggles, the black or marbled pages, the index fingers, though they may not always amuse us, at least serve to remind us that the image reflected in the mirror is less real than the mirror itself: that the mirror, not the reflections in it, has priority of status.

Many of Sterne's other typographical usages also serve to call us back from the show to the showman. Italics, for example, enact the actor's emphasis—the raised voice, the confidential whisper, or the wink; while capitals and gothic letters supply heavier emphasis for a moral reflection, a scholarly reference, or a tear. Asterisks and blank spaces similarly provoke our active response, and lead us to ask what they stand for, or to supply something for ourselves, whether correctly or not we often don't quite know; they are the graphic equivalents of the figure of aposiopesis—rhetorically intentional hiatus—which Tristram so often employs. Faint but pursuing, we do our best to puzzle out the asterisks and fill up the gaps; and we are occasionally given the ostentatiously grudging reward which the professional stage performer usually bestows on the unfortunate amateur from the audience who has offered his cooperation. For instance, when Walter and Toby have been left halfway down stairs, and Tristram wants to start the next scene with Walter back in bed, he turns to us with patronizing indulgence: "——So then, friend! You have got my father and my uncle *Toby* off the stairs, and seen them to bed?——And how did you manage it?——You dropped a curtain at the stair-foot——I thought you had no other way for it——Here's a crown for your trouble" (4, 13).

As to the particular roles Tristram assumes in his address to the reader, they are as varied as his moods. He often seeks to excite pathos, but in different ways: as a Shandy baby he invites commiseration for the early catastrophes of his life; his appeal is more deeply felt and less ironic when he shares with us his mature recollections of his father and his uncle; and there are other times when the Shandy story is forgotten and he implores our pity merely as an author who has just been battered by critics and reviewers. But of course pathos is only one of Tristram's moods, and it usually ends with a smile as he asks us: "Pray reach me my fool's cap" and reassumes his favorite pose—the jester's.

As regards his psychological relationship to his audience, Tristram has many tricks for provoking an active and emotionally charged participation, besides his various ways of keeping us guessing. His main gambit is the traditional one of divide and rule. The audience is imagined to comprise various groups of which the most vocal are a miscellaneous collection of unsympathetic auditors against whom, in mere self-defense, Tristram has to mobilize the rest of his hearers. There are the great Lords who demand submission and dedications; there are solemn critics, pedants, Dutch commentators, church dignitaries, and men of civic substance, who are usually addressed with mock deference as "Your Worships" or "Your Reverences." Equally hostile, and even more threatening, are the censorious prudes; always on the lookout for scandal and obscenity, they are usually addressed as "Madam"; and the appellation nearly always serves as a signal to the reader that there is some dubious imputation in the air. The only morally unobjectionable way of drawing our attention to such bawdy, of course, is to deny it with obtrusive indignation. Thus, for instance, when Tristram has mentioned Jenny as "his friend," he at once has "Madam" challenge his description of the relationship:

> Friend!——My friend.——Surely, Madam, a friendship between the two sexes may subsist, and be supported without——Fy! Mr. *Shandy*:——Without any thing, Madam, but that tender and delicious sentiment, which ever mixes in friendship, where there is a difference of sex. Let me intreat you to study the pure and sentimental parts of the best *French* Romances;——It will really, Madam, astonish you to see with what a variety of chaste expressions this delicious sentiment, which I have the honour to speak of, is dressed out. (1, 18)

In this passage we also have an example of the exploitation of imaginary differences between different parts of the audience; for if there are insufferably dull and hostile characters around, there are also a few close friends, some of them imaginary, like Jenny, others real, like Eugenius and Garrick; and the reader, alarmed at the possibility that he might be numbered among the priggish and the pretentious, strives his utmost to achieve the perfect sympathetic understanding which will allow him to be enrolled in the charmed circle of Mr. Shandy's friends, a circle where, as a bonus, he will be on nodding terms with the great Mr. Pitt, and even join in Tristram's patronizing rejoinders to St. Thomas Aquinas and "Mr. Horace."

Among this ideal audience benevolence and good humor reign; and compelling the reader to adopt this mood was half Sterne's battle in achieving other literary effects. Aristotle pointed out that people don't normally laugh when they are alone, as readers usually are; so it is an essential prerequisite of Sterne's humor that he should create the sense of an active and friendly relation between himself and his audience, especially the unprudish and benevolent members of it; they must be brought to strain every nerve to achieve that *dies praeclarum* when they will be accepted as close friends by Mr. Shandy. For reasons further clarified by a remark in the pseudo-Aristotelian *Problemata*: "Why are people less able to restrain their laughter in the presence of friends? Is it because, when anything is especially elated, it is easier set into motion? Now benevolence causes elation, so that laughter more easily moves us."

For Sterne and his readers, benevolence meant, above all, a readiness to shed a sympathetic tear. The Le Fever passage may be taken as an illustration of how the flow of feeling also helps Tristram's humorous designs; it also, of course, raises the oft-mooted question of whether the climactic comic twists Sterne habitually gives to sentimental episodes means that he is really attacking or ridiculing the pathetic and benevolent feelings he so often arouses and indeed seems to applaud.

In the passage about Le Fever's death, for example, reader and author were deeply united in the fellowship of suffering before they pulled back to smile at the unexpected reality which their joint imaginings had momentarily assumed: "Shall I go on? —— No." Community in commiseration is a precondition of community in merriment, Sterne seems to affirm. Our age tends to a circumspect gravity as well about life as about literature, which probably makes it difficult to fully appreciate Sterne's attitude. But we must remember that the eighteenth century's growing approval of humor runs exactly parallel to the growth of its cult of sentiment and benevolence. And not only chronologically: Shaftesbury and Hutcheson were the great precursors of both trends; and we can now see that the growing approval of laughter, and of emotional responsiveness in general, may be regarded as parallel manifestations of the dethronement of reason as the primary human faculty.

Sterne's humor, it may be said, largely depends upon the force of this dual exploitation of man's sympathetic and risible faculties. In Restoration comedy, or in Swift and Pope, we think not so much of humor as of wit; behind the epigrammatic brilliance we sense a mocking rejection of the objects satirized; and if emotions are aroused, they are the negative ones — scorn, distrust, hatred. This was in keeping both with Hobbes's view of the aggressive function of laughter, and with the neoclassical critical theory whereby the aim of satire was to mobilize the reader's feelings against illusion, affectation, and vice.

But in *Tristram Shandy* there is no vice; illusion and affectation are there, of course, but they are fantastic, amusing, and even, in their way, necessary: as with Walter and Toby, for instance, they are merely hobbyhorses. It's relevant here to observe that "hobby," in the sense of a favorite pastime, acquired its modern approbative sense only in the nineteenth century; originally it was a hobbyhorse, or an imitation horse, such as was used in the mummers' dance or as a child's toy; so a concern with hobbyhorses in an adult had, to an earlier generation, seemed a frivolous derogation of man's stature as a rational animal. But Sterne welcomed all such toys; he was willing to approve "an uncle Toby's siege — or an *any thing*, which a man makes a shift to get a-stride on, to canter it away from the cares and solicitudes of life."

A special stylistic strategy was required to express the coexistence of humor and sentiment, and indeed of a very large diversity of attitudes, in a context that did not impose or imply a rationally ordered hierarchy of values. This can perhaps be best illustrated by comparison. The typical epigram, like the typical sentence, goes in one direction. When the Lincolnshire lady was ill-advised enough to show Dr. Johnson her underground grotto, and then inquired "if he did not think it would be a pretty convenient habitation?", Dr. Johnson retorted: "I think it would, Madam, for a toad." Either you're for houses or you're for grottoes; Johnson's wit directs our attention to the incompatibility between the categories. Sterne's outlook, on the other hand, is much more pluralist, and so is his style. His ostentatiously permissive syntax allows each category its own independent existence; the dash makes no assertion of relation, but allows the sense to flow forwards and backwards between the phrases which it conjoins, very much at the reader's pleasure; the emphasis is up to us, and if there is exclusion, it is we who make it. Tristram, we feel, would have answered the Lincolnshire lady's query so as to leave open all the diverse possibilities on both sides; perhaps by saying "I *think* it would, Madam — for us — or — for a toad."

This sort of intentional leaving of the final evaluative attitude up to the audience is a very common technique in the stage comic; Mort Sahl is only the most extreme example of a style which depends entirely on the unstructured, parenthetic conjunction of diverse propositions and attitudes. At a much more highly controlled and complex level, we get an equally free choice in *Tristram Shandy*. Shakespeare's Yorick was a jester in a tragedy. Sterne's Yorick affirms a more programmatic kind of coexistence: sentiment and humor—and much else—should be regarded, however illogically, as somehow mutually consistent categories; we reject at our peril the exclusive claims either of the heart or of the head, or, for that matter, of the imagination, even if they seem to be in conflict.

At this point it is perhaps worth insisting that his open-ended mode of writing is very different in aim from such modern manipulations of point of view as "interior monologue" or "stream of consciousness." For "stream of consciousness" is normally supposed to be the expression of the unconscious and inarticulate flow of impressions, whereas Tristram is surely highly self-conscious and obtrusively articulate. Sterne would seem to agree with Locke that an unconscious idea is a contradiction in terms, and deals mainly with conscious, and indeed rationally conceptualized, matters. In addition Tristram's thoughts are quite overtly addressed to an audience, whereas stream of consciousness pretends that the reader does not exist. The stream of consciousness, in fact, takes the inner world of the individual character to the extreme limit of subjective realism; while Tristram's rhetoric is largely devoted to subverting the literal reality of fiction so that the reader's attention shall be focused on the reality not of the narrative but of the narrator.

Some critics, it is true, have seen the total of Tristram's reminiscences—that is, the whole book—as constituting a subjective individual portrait, much as Joyce and Proust portray their characters by presenting their inner thoughts. But although there is nothing exactly out of character in Tristram's thoughts, they surely don't seem aimed at indirect character portrayal. Rather, the apparently rather random association of thoughts in Tristram's discourse surely reflects a comic exploration of the extremely varied possibilities of Locke's view of pathological mental processes. Faced with the observation that "There is scarce any one that does not observe something that seems odd to him, and is in itself really extravagant, in the opinions, reasonings, and actions of other men," Locke explained that such failures of the human understanding result from the irrational association of ideas.

In the opening passage, we have a classical example of Mrs. Shandy's association of ideas between the dual monthly routines of Mr. Shandy in his timekeeping and his connubial roles. But there is nothing very unconscious about this in the modern sense; Pavlov's dog, had it the gift of tongues, would, under similar circumstances, have echoed Mrs. Shandy's words. In any case Sterne's emphasis is not on exploring the preconscious or unconscious mind of Mrs. Shandy so much as on using a logically inappropriate conjunction of ideas for comic purposes; and these comic purposes depend upon the reader's being keenly alive to the rational and conscious level of discourse from which Mrs. Shandy deviates.

Tristram's voice is by no means an irrational one, but a rational instrument for the revelation of human irrationality. Belonging to the Age of Reason helped Sterne to see and demonstrate that human behavior is not based on reason; in the end Locke had taught him, not so much that the human mind is a blank tablet, as that philosophical attempts to transcend ordinary human experience end up in a blind alley.

On the other hand, Sterne is as far from the intellectual satire of Swift as he is from the stream of consciousness, because his account of the non-rational aspects of human behavior does not condemn them. Sterne is as committed to the realities of the feelings and of the senses as he is to the life of the mind; he doesn't commit himself to the prior claims of reason and order, as wit and satire usually tends to do.

Here we can find abundant support in recent scholarship, in John Traugott's *Tristram Shandy's World* (Berkeley and Los Angeles, 1954) for instance, or in Ernest Tuveson's *The Imagination as a Means of Grace* (Berkeley and Los Angeles, 1960), for seeing *Tristram Shandy* as the most inclusive literary expression of a movement whose greatest philosophical representative is David Hume. Faced by the apparent failure of man to live up to his alleged nature as a rational animal, and forced to be dubious about the probability of success in Locke's effort to tidy matters up, this movement turned its attention to the complexities of actual human behavior and to the mysteries of psychological identification between individuals. Tristram's personal "Essay concerning Human Understanding" showed that understanding, if it came at all, came not through the rational faculty, nor through ordinary verbal communication, but through the operation of sympathy and imagination — the two faculties which were beginning to replace the traditional duality of passion and reason as the primary elements in man's understanding of his nature. Tristram's voice, if we attend to it, does not merely direct our attention to the traditional subject of comedy — human folly; it also suggests that we must go beyond the premature exclusions to which the rational mind's awareness of irrationality is always prompting us, and enlarge the area of our imaginative sympathy.

Consider, for example, Trim's great harangue on mortality, in which Tristram's directing presence deftly combines humor and pathos, and defies us to reject any of the human inconsistencies involved. Susannah the chambermaid, Jonathan the coachman, Obadiah the outdoor servant, the unnamed cookmaid, and the foolish fat scullion, are all gathered in the kitchen after hearing the news of the death of Bobby, Tristram's elder brother. Jonathan has just remarked that Bobby "was alive last Whitsuntide":

> ——O *Jonathan!* 'twould make a good-natured man's heart bleed, to consider, continued the corporal (standing perpendicularly), how low many a brave and upright fellow has been laid since that time! ——And trust me, *Susy,* added the corporal, turning to *Susannah,* whose eyes were swimming in water, ——before that time comes round again, ——many a bright-eye will be dim. ——*Susannah* placed it to the right side of the page——she wept——but she court'sied too. ——Are we not, continued *Trim,* looking still at *Susannah*——are we not like a flower of the field——a tear of pride stole in betwixt every two tears of humiliation——else no tongue could have described *Susannah's* affliction——is not all flesh grass? ——'Tis clay, ——'tis dirt. ——They all looked directly at the scullion, ——the scullion had just been scouring a fish-kettle. —— It was not fair. ——
>
> ——What is the finest face that ever man looked at! ——I could hear *Trim* talk so for ever, cried *Susannah,* ——what is it! (*Susannah* laid her hand upon *Trim's* shoulder)——but corruption? —— *Susannah* took it off.
>
> Now I love you for this——and 'tis this delicious mixture within you which makes you dear creatures what you are——and he who hates you for it——all I can say of the matter is——That he has either a pumpkin for his head——or a pippin for his heart, —— and whenever he is dissected 'twill be found so. (5, 9)

We find it difficult to decide what are the appropriate criteria for the indeterminate literary genres, the kinds of writing where the total literary structure is an aggregate rather than an organic whole. Formally, as Northrop Frye has suggested, *Tristram Shandy* may be regarded as a hybrid between the novel and the Menippean satire, or, as he prefers to call the genre, an Anatomy, like the works of two of Sterne's great forebears, Rabelais and Burton.

But if we must decide not so much the fictional category, as the primary principle of unity, of *Tristram Shandy*, it must surely be Tristram's voice. Through it Sterne discovered a principle of order which resides not so much in linear development in time as in a kind of timeless consistency of texture; it is this which has primary autonomy, and which controls every narrative element, from the phrase to the paragraph, the chapter, and the book. So, by the "comic syntax of *Tristram Shandy*," I mean only that the syntax, "the orderly or systematic arrangements of parts or elements" as the *Oxford Dictionary* defines it, of *Tristram Shandy*, is essentially a complex but consistent mode of comic speech which unites all its parts and attitudes, loosely no doubt, but with perfect appropriateness (this mode of speech is perhaps strictly speaking more humorous than comic, but my title defers to the trochaic rhythm of Sterne's). In any case it is this voice which joins the novelistic to the more miscellaneous elements of the book; which unites the pathetic and the laughable, the intellectual and the emotional; and which, above all, engages the author and the reader in so living a conversation that one no longer asks, as one does of a novel, for an ending.

Yeats called art "the social act of a solitary man." Sterne was a solitary; but toward the end of his life he found a way of talking which created its own society. The members of this society, comprising both the fictional characters in the book, its circle of readers, and its narrator, all have a very special literary quality; their voices are attuned to the endless dialogue within, which is so much more inconsequential, indecent, and above all—shall we face it—trivial, than the public dialogues we can hear going on around us, or that we find recorded in most of literature; Sterne's sad recognition of this enabled him to create a mode of speech which compels what he most desired—our acknowledgment of intimate kinship. And once the Shandean laughter has punctured the authorized hyperboles which make it so difficult for us to recognize our real identity, the remembering mind can sometimes go on beyond this to discover in and through Tristram's comic syntax that real feeling and a kind of logic somehow subsist and trace a shadowy coherence upon the muddled and miscellaneous indignities of our personal lot.

Sterne: The Poetics of Sensibility

Martin Battestin

Well into his ninth and final volume, Tristram Shandy openly invites comparison of his autobiography with Swift's equally zany masterpiece, claiming an immortality for his *Life and Opinions* as deserved as that which "the *Legation of Moses,* or the *Tale of a Tub*" will enjoy. In this, as "Posterity" has proved by confirming half the prediction, he was a better prophet than Dr. Johnson, for, though sufficiently "odd" by neoclassical standards, *Tristram Shandy* has lasted. Indeed—to apply a more recent standard of literary merit, no less infallible—it appears in retrospect the most "relevant" production of the age, the age which marked, as Leo Spitzer put it, "the great caesura" between the old ideology and the new. It was Sterne, Earl Wasserman observes, not Johnson or Burke or Gibbon, who sensed most surely the intellectual currents stirring in the latter half of the eighteenth century, currents that soon enough would sweep away the traditional grounds of faith and morality which had nourished and, as we have seen, in a sense determined the forms of art.

From the viewpoint of Augustan aesthetics, certainly, *Tristram Shandy* and *A Tale of a Tub* seem "odd" in similar ways. As a narrator, Tristram is as obstinate as the Teller in straying from the straight road: there are so many irresistible "views and prospects" that beckon him, and he "will not balk" his fancy for the mean considerations of method and regularity. His style, too, is "wild," a rhapsody of broken sentences, interjections, interruptions, nonsequiturs—in short, a philosopher's nightmare. For Hume at midcentury, as earlier for Hobbes and Swift, prose such as this, lacking all order

From *The Providence of Wit: Aspects of Form in Augustan Literature and the Arts.* © 1974 by Martin C. Battestin. University Press of Virginia. 1974.

and design, resembled "the ravings of a madman." Tristram also seems to share with the Teller the conviction that men are irrational, creatures more of the senses than of the spirit:

> I said, "we are not stocks and stones" — 'tis very well. I should have added, nor are we angels, I wish we were, — but men cloathed with bodies, and governed by our imaginations; — and what a junketting piece of work of it there is, betwixt these and our seven senses, especially some of them, for my own part, I own it, I am ashamed to confess.

"REASON is," for him, "half of it, SENSE." For Swift, as we have seen, this was the fatal syndrome of Modernism, the disease of an age whose idols were self and the body; and the Teller, who personifies these corruptions of the Christian humanist ideal, is the object of his author's devastating mockery. In *Tristram Shandy,* however, the ethos that informed Swift's irony has given way to a new understanding of the human condition for which the appropriate literary response is no longer satire, but farce and pathos. It is because he is a "modern" man that Tristram Shandy—like Sterne, like his reader—is a "small HERO," "the continual sport of what the world calls Fortune." Not pride, but the mind itself isolates the Shandys within themselves; not reason, but the heart and senses and imagination offer the hope of release and communion. In the different attitudes of Swift and Sterne to method and confusion, judgement and fancy, mind and body, we may discern the passing of traditional values and the emergence of a new conception, based on a new definition of human nature, of the ways in which the literary artist imitates life. As eccentric in its architecture (whose unevenness annoys Walter, the man of reason) as in the lives of its inhabitants, Shandy Hall is the theatre of the modern world.

It is not, of course, "modern" in all its appearances. For one thing, the Shandys themselves profess to believe in a providential universe. To Toby, the pious warrior, "providence brings good out of everything," even gunpowder; and the Deity is both "the Father" of compassion, and the perfect judge whose wisdom will at last distinguish the hypocrite from the honest man. Man in affliction, he counsels Walter, despondent over the accident to Tristram's nose, is "upheld by the grace and the assistance of the best of Beings." Even Walter, to whom such religious comforts merely cut "the knot" of life's tangled skein when an ingenious hypothesis or two might untie it, can use a Christian argument on occasion. And Tristram, though he doubts, shrewdly enough, that the Christian religion will survive another half century, pays his respects to "the Disposer of all things," whose "infinite wisdom . . . dispenses every thing," including the proportions of wit and judgement in the human mind, "in exact weight and measure."

But what is remarkable, and finally ominous, about Tristram's auto-biography is that in it the Shandys, good and faithful Christians though they may be, are seen to inhabit a world defined in *human* terms alone. The idea of Providence that helped to determine the special character of *Tom Jones* and *The Vicar of Wakefield* as works of art is in *Tristram Shandy* merely incidental and perfunctory. The Shandys act out the bumbling comedy of their lives not against the generous and reassuring background of cosmic Order, but within a frame as constricted as a country parish and as muddled as the mind of man. Their "world," like that of the village midwife, is no more "than a small circle described upon the circle of the great world, of four *English* miles diameter, or thereabouts, of which the cottage where the good old woman lived, is supposed to be the centre"—a circle, Tristram continues, "of which kind every soul living, whether he has a shirt to his back or no,—has one surrounding him." In *Tristram Shandy* not Nature or Nature's God, but the self is the hub of the universe. This was the lesson that, first among contemporary novelists, Sterne drew from Locke, whose "glory" it was "to free the world from the lumber of a thousand vulgar errors." Since, as Locke argued, there are no innate ideas, it might be seen to follow that our ap-prehension of the world, and therefore our understanding of ourselves, will be relative and problematical, differing for each individual according to his experience. Nature, which Pope and his fellow Augustans had regarded as "One *clear, unchang'd,* and *Universal* Light"—the "just Standard" by which reasonable men regulated their lives and the ideal pattern for the artist's imitation—could now no longer be confidently regarded as an objective and uniform phenomenon, divinely ordained and for all men at all times "still the same." Reality is now no longer something external to the individual—something "out there" to which he must relate in prescribed ways; it has become internal and subjective, a world, as it were, of his own involuntary creating whose tenuous order, imposed by the mechanical operations of the mind organizing a multiplicity of sensations, is for each man private and arbitrary and unique.

This is one implication of Sterne's epigraph from Epictetus: "It is not things themselves that disturb men, but their judgments about these things." As the title page warns us, we are not to expect adventures and certainties in this book, but the life and especially the *opinions* of one individual man, "Tristram Shandy, Gentleman." *Tom Jones* and *The Vicar of Wakefield* may be read as paradigm and parable because they were written from the convic-tion that Truth, like human nature, is one and ever the same, that the drama of each individual life, however unique in its particular circumstances, recapitulates the drama of the human condition in general unfolding under the eye of Providence. Through the "Individual" Fielding implies the "Species." Though Tristram expects his book to be "no less read than the *Pilgrim's Progress* itself," his own life is no allegory because there is no longer any common system of belief, no "higher" reality beyond itself, to which it can relate. If Vanity Fair was Bunyan's emblem for the world, whose proper character all men might recognize if they would, for Tristram the metaphor has another significance, connoting the separateness and relativism of life: "every man will speak of the fair as his own market has gone in it; — for which cause I affirm it over again to be one of the vilest worlds that ever was made." The world is indeed a different and ultimately a private place for each of the Shandys. By his own admission, Tristram is "a most tragicomical completion of his [father's] prediction, 'That I should neither think, nor act like any other man's child.' " Walter, too, is unique, his peculiar angle of vision distorting his perception of the world so that he becomes, in effect, the creator of his own private universe:

> The truth was, his road lay so very far on one side, from that wherein most men travelled, — that every object before him presented a face and section of itself to his eye, altogether different from the plan and elevation of it seen by the rest of mankind. — In other words, 'twas a different object, — and in course was differently considered.

Our "preconceptions," Tristram observes as Toby misconstrues another of his brother's metaphors, have "as great a power over the sounds of words as the shapes of things." The most explicit statement in the novel of this subjectivism, however, is Walter's dissertation on time and duration, that invaluable, though regrettably abortive, contribution to "the *Ontologic treasury*" which he has borrowed from Locke:

> *For if you will turn your eyes inwards upon your mind,* continued my father, *and observe attentively, you will perceive, brother, that whilst you and I are talking together, and thinking and smoking our pipes: or whilst we receive successively ideas in our minds, we know that we do exist, and so we estimate the existence, or the continuation of the existence of ourselves, or any thing else commensurate to the succession of any ideas in our minds, the duration of ourselves, or any such other thing, co existing with our thinking, — and so according to that preconceived* — You puzzle me to death, cried my uncle *Toby.* —

The Shandys find life puzzling in more ways than one. It remains an enigma despite Walter's hypotheses or Toby's simple piety or Tristram's desperate efforts to encompass it within the nine volumes of his autobiography:

> But mark, madam, we live amongst riddles and mysteries — the most obvious things, which come in our way, have dark sides, which the quickest sight cannot penetrate into; and even the clearest and most exalted understandings amongst us find ourselves puzzled and at a loss in almost every cranny of nature's works.

Though a different place for each of them, the world bears nevertheless a common aspect: inexplicable even when it appears most obvious, overwhelming in its multiplicity, unpredictable in its contingencies, it bewilders and eludes them all — and they themselves, as Tristram protests to the commissary at Lyons, are the heart of the enigma:

> — My good friend, quoth I — as sure as I am I — and you are you —
> — And who are you? said he. — Don't puzzle me; said I.

In *Tristram Shandy* traditional explanations of the human condition have given way to a distinctly "modern" view of man based on Lockean epistemology. As *Tom Jones* is the fictional embodiment of the Augustan ethos most memorably articulated in *An Essay on Man*, Sterne's remarkable book is the objectification in art of the new subjectivism implicit in *An Essay concerning Human Understanding*, the work that Tristram calls "a history-book . . . of what passes in a man's own mind" and that his author valued next to the Bible. However orthodox he may have been as a priest, as a novelist Sterne conceived the curse of Adam not in Christian terms, according to the Augustinian doctrine of innate depravity, but in terms of the new philosophy: as the nature of the mind itself, whose mechanism, beyond our power to control, limits our knowledge of the world to our experience of it, isolating the individual within the prison of the self. Solipsism, which for Swift or Fielding, let us say, is the consequence of pride and self-love, is for Sterne a condition of life which can be mitigated neither by the will nor by the reason, but by feeling and the imagination. The mind itself has become the marplot of Eden. Mechanically associating "ideas which have no connection in nature" — ideas such as the winding of a clock and the act of sexual intercourse — it inhibits, at times prevents, communion and relationship with other human beings. From one point of view, the hilarious opening chapter of *Tristram Shandy* may be seen as Sterne's arch reinterpretation of the Augustinian doctrine that the Children are victimized by the mistakes of the Parents:

it is not "sin" which spoils Tristram's conception—"the effects of which I fear I shall carry with me to my grave"—but the mind, its irksome mechanism of confinement and frustration:

> *Pray, my dear,* quoth my mother, *have you not forgot to wind up the clock?*——*Good G*——*!* cried my father, making an exclamation, but taking care to moderate his voice at the same time,—— *Did ever woman, since the creation of the world, interrupt a man with such a silly question?*

Intercourse of a verbal kind is equally unsatisfactory, Sterne implies, either because of the dullness of our understandings—for which reason Walter's conversation with his wife in their "Bed of Justice" is as one-sided as any Socratic dialogue—or because of the mind's tendency to draw from language only those meanings and connotations which conform to our private prejudices and predispositions. Toby, for example, conditioned past all redeeming to a world of armaments and fortifications, is as apt a demonstration of Bergson's theory of comedy as one could wish. The mechanism of his brain registers only those snatches of discourse that relate to his obsession:

> Now, whether we observe it or no, continued my father, in every sound man's head, there is a regular succession of ideas of one sort or other, which follow each other in train just like—— A train of artillery? said my uncle *Toby.*—— A train of a fiddlestick!—— quoth my father,——

Responding in conversation by preconditioned reflexes, Toby might serve as a case study from B. F. Skinner's notebook. Dr. Slop's sudden arrival inevitably brings Stevinus to his mind. Walter's contortions while reaching for his pocket with his opposite hand remind his brother of the returning angle of the traverse where he incurred his wound at Namur. As Walter, lamenting the accident to Tristram's nose, asks, "did ever a poor unfortunate man . . . receive so many lashes?" Toby recalls the flogging of a grenadier in Makay's regiment. As Yorick in an unguarded moment uses the phrase "point blank" metaphorically, Toby rises "to say something upon projectiles." Though he is the soul of complaisance and wishes to be attentive to please his brother, Toby's mind will not turn upon any subject alien to his private experience and preoccupations. His fancy strays to the bowling green as Walter lectures upon Prignitz, but it returns, "quick as a note could follow the touch," when he hears the word "siege."

Toby is only the most notable instance in the novel of Sterne's view that men are governed not by reason, but by their imagination, which is in turn conditioned by sensuous experience—by those circumstances in life which wound us or give us pleasure. Noting that a thin man like himself must see the world differently from a corpulent philosopher such as Bishop Hall, Tristram professes to admire the Pythagoreans, who sought a life of pure ratiocination; but he is aware that there is no escape from the body, that our estimation of things, our thoughts and our ideals, are determined by our humours and appetites:

> I love the *Pythagoreans* (much more than ever I dare tell my dear *Jenny*) for their . . . *"getting out of the body, in order to think well."* No man thinks right whilst he is in it; blinded, as he must be, with his congenial humours, and drawn differently aside, as the bishop and myself have been, with too lax or too tense a fibre— REASON is, half of it, SENSE; and the measure of heaven itself is but the measure of our present appetites and concoctions—

This passage is at the heart of Sterne's philosophy of human life and character in *Tristram Shandy*. He sees the mind as not only imprisoned in the body, but controlled by it—our apprehension of the world and of ourselves determined by our senses. His metaphor for this fact is the Hobbyhorse, at once the source of our limitations and frustrations (and therefore of much of the novel's comedy), and a means of our survival in a vexing and incomprehensible world. As Tristram assures us in dedicating his autobiography to the highest bidder, the Hobbyhorse is "a kind of background to the whole." Superficially at least, Sterne's notion of the Hobbyhorse seems only another, more whimsical version of the theory of the ruling passion popular in contemporary psychology and most memorably stated in Pope's *Epistle to Cobham* and the *Essay on Man*. "WHEN a man," Tristram observes, "gives himself up to the government of a ruling passion, — or, in other words, when his HOBBY-HORSE grows head-strong, — farewell cool reason and fair discretion!" If we would know the characters of men, Pope's advice is to "Search then the Ruling Passion." Accordingly, Tristram "will draw my uncle *Toby's* character from his HOBBY-HORSE."

Both concepts apparently lend themselves to a deterministic view of human nature: we do not choose to be driven by the appetites that motivate our actions. In the Christian humanist tradition, however, as it was understood by Pope and Swift and Fielding, the passions may be governed by reason and the will, bringing the self into conformity with moral norms divinely sanctioned and accepted by society. In *Tristram Shandy*, on the other hand, the notion of the Hobbyhorse does not function in an ethical, but rather in an epistemological and ontological context, as the vehicle for the relativist view of reality which Sterne found to be implicit in Locke's subjectivism. Walter's hypotheses, Toby's military games, Tristram's obsession with capturing his life on paper—each is the manifestation of the mind's instinctive attempt to organize experience, to impose on the painful and disconcerting multiplicity of things an order and a meaning it otherwise would lack. The order his Hobbyhorse affords is real enough and necessary to the rider, but in an absolute sense it is illusory and, as a guide to life, continually belied by intractable circumstances and contingencies. In *A Tale of a Tub* this habit of mind is equivalent to madness, for Swift, like those other Augustans we have been considering, believed that the Order of things was objectively founded, and discernible to the eye of reason. But if, as Bacon implied, the old cosmology was itself a kind of hobbyhorsical construct testifying to man's natural inclination to organize actuality according to his preconceptions; and if, as Locke reasoned, there are no innate ideas, no one and universal conception of reality—then, in Swift's sense, we are all system builders inhabiting private worlds of our own imagining. In *Tristram Shandy* for the first time in English fiction, Sterne explored these implications of the new philosophy.

His attitude toward the Hobbyhorse is ambivalent. On the one hand, it is an obsession narrowing the range of possible responses to life and, as it affects our relationships with others, potentially destructive. On the other hand, it is the mind's defence against the bewildering and often inimical world that threatens to overwhelm us. Controlling our perception of the world, the Hobbyhorse limits and distorts reality, completing the process of self-enclosure which the mechanism of the mind already assures. Walter's way, as Tristram remarks, "was to force every event in nature into an hypothesis, by which means never man crucified TRUTH at the rate he did." And as Walter's continually abortive efforts to converse with his brother or "hang up" inferences within his wife's "head-piece" make clear, the Hobbyhorse cooperates with other causes (stupidity, for example) to prevent communication. In *Tristram Shandy*, as Rebecca West has somewhere observed of life, there are no dialogues, only intersecting monologues. Happiness, Swift ironically declared in *A Tale of a Tub,* is "*a perpetual Possession of being well Deceived.*" In *Tristram Shandy* Sterne in effect accepts that definition, for the mind as he sees it, being limited by its dependence on the senses, must find contentment if at all only in a partial and imperfect vision of a world too vast to comprehend, too enigmatic to explain. Our Hobbyhorses are based on the delusion—but a delusion necessary to enable us to function at all—that the order we impose on the world and in terms of which we govern and solace our lives, is equivalent to Truth, that our private ontologies may substitute for Reality.

They are, therefore, inevitably a source of our discomfiture, and of Sterne's droll estimation of the farce of life. Walter, whose only happiness is the conviction that he may control the world with an ingenious hypothesis, is perpetually disappointed by circumstances:

> Will not the gentle reader pity my father from his soul? — to
> see an orderly and well-disposed gentleman, who tho' singular,
> — yet inoffensive in his notions, — so played upon in them by
> cross purposes; — to look down upon the stage, and see him baf-
> fled and overthrown in all his little systems and wishes; to behold
> a train of events perpetually falling out against him, and in so
> critical and cruel a way, as if they had purposedly been plann'd
> and pointed against him, merely to insult his speculations. — In
> a word, to behold such a one, in his old age, ill-fitted for troubles,
> ten times in a day suffering sorrow; — ten times in a day calling
> the child of his prayers TRISTRAM! — Melancholy dissyllable of
> sound! which, to his ears, was unison to *Nincompoop*, and every
> name vituperative under heaven. — By his ashes! I swear it, —
> if ever malignant spirit took pleasure, or busied itself by travers-
> ing the purposes of mortal man, — it must have been here; —

Tristram himself must admit the hopelessness of his own efforts to bend life to his wishes. A year after he completed the first instalment of his autobiography, Tristram, "having got . . . almost into the middle of my fourth volume — and no farther than to my first day's life," recognizes that he cannot make his pen keep pace with time: "as at this rate I should just live 364 times faster than I should write — It must follow, an' please your worships, that the more I write, the more I shall have to write." Our Hobbyhorses, furthermore, however innocently we mount them, not only increase our own frustrations, but prove troublesome to others. Dr. Slop's darling forceps, Toby's requiring the lead weights of window sashes to cast his toy cannons, Walter's teaching that names and noses have magical powers over the lives of men — all have their awkward and debilitating consequences for Tristram:

> Unhappy *Tristram*! child of wrath! child of decrepitude! interrup-
> tion! mistake! and discontent! What one misfortune or disaster
> in the book of embryotic evils, that could unmechanize thy frame,
> or entangle thy filaments! which has not fallen upon thy head,
> or ever thou camest into the world — what evils in thy passage
> into it! — What evils since! —

Paradoxically, though it limits and annoys, the Hobbyhorse is also our solace and compensation in a puzzling, injurious world. However absurd and fugitive its pleasures, however inadequate as a means to Truth, it is for each of the Shandys his stay against confusion:

> 'Tis the sporting little filly-folly which carries you out for the present hour — a maggot, a butterfly, a picture, a fiddle-stick — an uncle *Toby's* siege — or an *any thing*, which a man makes a shift to get a stride on, to canter it away from the cares and solicitudes of life — 'Tis as useful a beast as is in the whole creation — nor do I really see how the world could do without it —

As Walter sees it, and as it functions in the lives of all the Shandys, it is something more than a temporary diversion from care; it is the expression of our instinctive desire to endure, to find compensations for the blows and disappointments life deals us. His hopes in Tristram's nose having been dashed, he will offset the evil by christening his son Trismegistus, thereby counterbalancing the failure of one favourite hypothesis by the prompt application of another. So, he observes to Toby, explaining man's resiliency in the "rugged journey" of life, there is a "great and elastic power within us of counterbalancing evil, which like a secret spring in a well-ordered machine, though it can't prevent the shock — at least it imposes upon our sense of it."

But it is Toby himself whose Hobbyhorse supplies the paradigm of this reflexive capacity of the mind to reduce life, the destructive element, to a form which may be mastered and enjoyed. Toby's obsession with model fortifications grew during his painful recuperation from the groin wound he received at the siege of Namur, and it is the means of his recovery. At first, frustrated in his attempt to beguile the pain of the wound by recounting the history of it, Toby aggravated rather than eased his condition. The inadequacy of language to recreate the experience so that it might be either shared by others or comprehended by himself compounds his perplexity and despair: "his life," as Tristram expresses it, "was put in jeopardy by words." Only by objectifying the experience — by turning from words to maps, so that he can "stick a pin upon the identical spot of ground where he was standing in when the stone struck him" — is he able to master and exorcise it; and this principle once learned he extends to all battles, the activity that once defined his life, procuring plans and histories of the fortified towns of Italy and France, "all which he would read with that intense application and delight, that he would forget himself, his wound, his confinement, his dinner." His wound is finally cured, however, only when the process of objectification is complete: contracting the theatre of war to the Lilliputian dimensions of a sheltered bowling green, Toby methodically reenacts Marlborough's campaigns, now towering over and safely controlling the violent world that injured him. Tristram's own Hobbyhorse similarly enables him to recreate, to objectify by committing to paper, the experiences of a life which he too, though a "small HERO," has found a kind of warfare upon earth, suffering the slings and arrows of Fortune—that "ungracious Duchess" who "in every stage of my life, and at every turn and corner where she could get fairly at me . . . has pelted me with a set of as pitiful misadventures and cross accidents as ever small HERO sustained." His books, he trusts,

> shall make its way in the world, much better than its master has done before it——Oh *Tristram*! *Tristram*! can this but be once brought about——the credit, which will attend thee as an author, shall counterbalance the many evils which have befallen thee as a man——thou wilt feast upon the one——when thou hast lost all sense and remembrance of the other!——

The Hobbyhorse, then, though a mixed blessing, is a way of ordering life and of coping with it. In a sense that delightfully anticipates more recent psychological theory, it is also a way of displacing and sublimating sexual urges that Sterne, rather like Freud, appears to have regarded as the common denominator of the human condition. If Toby's groin wound led to his obsession with military games, it was also the cause of the "extream and unparallel'd modesty" of his nature; he knows, as Walter remarks in exasperation, not "so much as the right end of a woman from the wrong." As he journeys, eager and blushing, to the country to take possession of his bowling green, Toby's Hobbyhorse seems surrogate for another kind of passion:

> Never did lover post down to a belov'd mistress with more heat and expectation, than my uncle *Toby* did, to enjoy this self-same thing in private; ——I say in private; ——for it was sheltered from the house, as I told you, by a tall yew hedge, and was covered on the other three sides, from mortal sight, by rough holly and thickset flowering shrubs; so that the idea of not being seen, did not a little contribute to the idea of pleasure preconceived in my uncle *Toby's* mind.

Only when the Treaty of Utrecht puts an end to his games on the green does Toby turn his attention to the Widow Wadman and begin "to lay siege to that fair and strong citadel." Though he takes no pleasure in sex, regarding a certain connubial office as a duty to be performed, as seldom as justice will allow, for the sake of posterity, Walter, too, can yet find rapture in a prologue on long noses: "when my father got home," Tristram relates, "he solaced himself with *Bruscambille* after the manner, in which, 'tis ten to one, your worship solaced yourself with your first mistress, — that is, from morning even unto night." As for Tristram, among "the many evils" which have befallen him "as a man" and for which his book must serve as compensation, we may recall the time he was left standing before his Jenny, garters in hand, "reflecting upon what had *not* pass'd"—a disaster "the most oppressive of its kind which could befall me as a man, proud, as he ought to be, of his manhood—."

None of the Shandys, not even Walter's bull, is very happy in sexual matters: they are interrupted, damaged in tender parts, impotent. The world the novel presents is one of frustration and misadventure in the most essential human relationship. Though Sterne is not quite to be regarded as a precursor of Lawrence, who seems to have shared Walter Shandy's opinion that "there is no passion so serious as lust," yet his sexual comedy is directly related to the novel's profoundest philosophical theme: the problem, implicit in Locke's epistemology, of human isolation, the imprisonment of the individual within the self. The solution to that problem, also implicit in Locke, Sterne found in the role the senses played in relating the self to the outside world, and in the emphasis on the social affections explicit in Shaftesbury and the Latitudinarian divines. Throughout *Tristram Shandy* the mind constricts, the senses enlarge the soul. Though an agile hypothesizer, Walter's efforts to make his brother understand him are frustrated rather than furthered by the dubious "gift of ratiocination and making syllogisms"; reason, indeed, is in one sense the measure of our fallen condition, "for in superior classes of beings, such as angels and spirits, — 'tis all done, may it please your worships, as they tell, by INTUITION." It is "the weakness and imbecility of human reason" that Sterne's comedy makes us conscious of, opposing the mechanical operations of the mind to the sure knowledge of the heart.

To translate the language of the heart, Tristram assures us as he ponders Slawkenbergius's tale of Diego and Julia, requires "a sixth sense":

> —— What can he mean by the lambent pupilability of slow, low, dry chat, five notes below the natural tone, —— which you know, madam, is little more than a whisper? The moment I pronounced the words, I could perceive an attempt towards a vibration in the strings, about the region of the heart. —— The brain made no acknowledgement. —— There's often no good understanding betwixt 'em. —— I felt as if I understood it. —— I had no ideas. —— The movement could not be without cause.

Sterne's reputation as a novelist of sentiment is, of course, founded on such passages. Not ratiocination but feeling, not discourse so much as moments of nonverbal, sensuous communion—a gesture, a caress, an attitude of body or a tone of voice—are the means to understanding. Of this the most famous example in the novel is "the lesson of universal good-will" that Tristram learns from Toby's kindness to a fly:

> I was but ten years old when this happened; — but whether it was, that the action itself was more in unison to my nerves at that age of pity, which instantly set my whole frame into one vibration of most pleasureable sensation; — or how far the manner and expression of it might go towards it; — or in what degree, or by what secret magick, — a tone of voice and harmony of movement, attuned by mercy, might find a passage to my heart, I know not; — this I know, that the lesson of universal good-will then taught and imprinted by my uncle *Toby*, has never since been worn out of my mind: And tho' I would not depreciate what the study of the *Literae humaniores*, at the university, have done for me in that respect, or discredit the other helps of an expensive education bestowed upon me, both at home and abroad since; — yet I often think that I owe one half of my philanthropy to that one accidental impression.

Tristram's analysis of how the experience affected him is reminiscent of the corporealism of Swift's Teller: Toby's action was "in unison" to his nerves, setting his "whole frame into one vibration"; its meaning was permanently "imprinted" on his mind. But here there is no irony intended. Reason for Sterne is, "half of it, SENSE," and the way to the soul is through the body. Though separated by their Hobbyhorses and by the general curse of self-enclosure, the Shandys are united in love and communicate through the unspoken language of the body: the tender glance that penetrates the heart, the clasp of hands, the tug of a garment, a whistle, a dance, the shedding of a tear—such are the means of communion in the novel, expressions of feeling that the senses convey directly to the heart.

This, surely, is one explanation—another being that he dearly loved a bawdy joke—for Sterne's apparent obsession with sexuality, the most intimate act of knowledge. In the final chapter of the novel, Walter's diatribe against man's sexual nature serves ironically as an apology for his author's theme and method:

> —THAT provision should be made for continuing the race of so great, so exalted and godlike a Being as man—I am far from

denying—but philosophy speaks freely of every thing; and therefore I still think and do maintain it to be a pity, that it should be done by means of a passion which bends down the faculties, and turns all the wisdom, contemplations, and operations of the soul backwards—a passion, my dear, continued my father, addressing himself to my mother, which couples and equals wise men and fools, and makes us come out of our caverns and hiding-places more like satyrs and four-footed beasts than men.

If the act of procreation is natural, he complains, why should it have offended the delicacy of philosophers and "wherefore, when we go about to make and plant a man, do we put out the candle?" Why are all its aspects and appurtenances "to be conveyed to a cleanly mind by no language, translation, or periphrasis whatever?" With society in general, Walter esteems the "act of killing and destroying a man" more "glorious," and the phallic instruments of war more "honourable":

—We march with them upon our shoulders—We strut with them by our sides—We gild them—We carve them—We inlay them—We enrich them—Nay, if it be but a *scoundril* cannon, we cast an ornament upon the breach of it.—

But Sterne is of another opinion and in *Tristram Shandy* intends, like Yorick, who has listened to Walter's reasoning with dismay, "to batter the whole hypothesis to pieces."

For the most part sensuality for the Shandys is a matter of embarrassment and frustration. Once, however, in the scene that closes Tristram's narrative of his race against death, it is the source of joy and harmony and communion, dispelling the curse of human limitation and mortality and providing Tristram a glimpse of Eden on the plains of Languedoc:

O! there is that sprightly frankness which at once unpins every plait of a *Languedocian's* dress—that whatever is beneath it, it looks so like the simplicity which poets sing of in better days —I will delude my fancy, and believe it is so.

As the scene unfolds, images that in the Augustan tradition had served as metaphors for Nature's abstract Order—the measured dance, the harmony of reconciled opposites—are humanized, rendering the love and concord in the hearts of men and women. Pope's Vulcan, the figure of the artist transforming a painful world into objects of ideal beauty, reappears, as it were, changed into the "lame youth, whom *Apollo* had recompenced with a pipe," providing simpler pleasures with a momentary music. At the sound, Tristram kicks off his boots and takes hold of Nanette's hands. "It taught me to forget I was a stranger." Her dress unpinned, her hair untied, they dance off as the nymphs and swains sing in harmony, affirming the joy of life and expelling sorrow—the meaning of his name:

> The sister of the youth who had stolen her voice from heaven, sung alternately with her brother——'twas a *Gascoigne* roundelay.
> VIVA LA JOIA!
> FIDON LA TRISTESSA!
> The nymphs join'd in unison, and their swains an octave below them——
>
> I would have given a crown to have it sew'd up——*Nanette* would not have given a sous——*Viva la joia!* was in her lips—— *Viva la joia!* was in her eyes. A transient spark of amity shot across the space betwixt us——

If only for the moment, Tristram is admitted to a world far from the clocks and Hobbyhorses of Shandy Hall, a world of innocent sensuality, free and vital, where there are no strangers.

The senses, then, are one means of relationship, the imagination is another. In his Preface, addressed to the "Anti-Shandeans" among his readers and placed with a Shandean disregard for logic in the midst of his third volume, Tristram hints at this view by disputing Locke's preference for judgement over wit in his analysis of the faculties of the mind. Though he freed the world from "a thousand vulgar errors," in this belief, Tristram insists, the philosopher was "bubbled." One reason for Sterne's criticism is apparent in Locke's definition of the two faculties, which represents judgement as working to separate "ideas wherein can be found the least difference" and wit as working to assemble "ideas . . . wherein can be found any resemblance." Judgement, in other words, dis-integrates; wit—for which "fancy" and "imagination" are synonymous terms—has "the opposite purpose of relating and combining the disparate elements of experience. In a world characterized by multiplicity and separateness, it is the mind's unifying power. In *Tristram Shandy*—through puns, analogues, metaphors, *double entendres* confusing ideas which the judgement would force apart—not the least of its functions is to heighten our sense that our sexual natures supply the common denominator of experience, that Sterne and his reader are joint participants in what Robert Alter has called "the game of love."

It is the imagination, furthermore, that unifies the world, relating the Self to the Other, and serves therefore to qualify the solipsism of Hobbes and Locke. For by imaginatively generalizing upon his own experience, the individual may escape the self, sharing emphatically in the happiness and distress of others and coming at last to the understanding that self-love and social are the same. In part, it is this sense of the individual's capacity for imaginative projection that informs the doctrines of good nature and universal benevolence which Shaftesbury and the Latitudinarians opposed to Hobbes and the Augustinian tradition. Sterne believed that both things were true: that if men were by nature self-enclosed and self-interested, they were also capable of communion, generosity, and love. Serving as an exemplum of this paradox is the scene in which Toby and Corporal Trim dispute whether a wound to the groin or one to the knee causes the more "intolerable anguish." The argument cannot be resolved rationally, since each man's experience of pain (or pleasure) is his only measure of what is real; but it can be dissolved into harmony by a higher principle:

> The dispute was maintained with amicable and equal force be-
> twixt my uncle *Toby* and *Trim* for some time; till *Trim* at length
> recollecting that he had often cried at his master's sufferings, but
> never shed a tear at his own — was for giving up the point, which
> my uncle *Toby* would not allow — 'Tis a proof of nothing, *Trim*,
> said he, but the generosity of thy temper —
> So that whether the pain of a wound in the groin (*cæteris paribus*)
> is greater than the pain of a wound in the knee — or
> Whether the pain of a wound in the knee is not greater than
> the pain of a wound in the groin — are points which to this day
> remain unsettled.

It is the mind's capacity imaginatively to make another's experience its own that defines the man of sensibility. For Walter, the "secret spring" that smooths the rough passages of life is his irrepressible Hobbyhorse; for Tristram, it is another sort of mechanism by which the happiness of others is made our own and colours our perception of the world, dissolving the boundaries that separate us and harmonizing the self and Nature:

> — For my uncle *Toby's* amours running all the way in my head,
> they had the same effect upon me as if they had been my own
> — I was in the most perfect state of bounty and good will; and
> felt the kindliest harmony vibrating within me, with every oscilla-
> tion of the chaise alike; so that whether the roads were rough
> or smooth, it made no difference; every thing I saw, or had to
> do with, touch'd upon some secret spring either of sentiment or
> rapture.

In this frame of mind Tristram encounters poor Maria. The compassion and benevolence he feels for her are genuine, but, as he is honest enough to sense, they are not his, or any man's, whole character. As he sits between Maria and her goat listening to her melancholy cadences, his sympathy for her sorrow is balanced by a less generous interest in her, making him aware "of what a *Beast* man is":

> MARIA look'd wistfully for some time at me, and then at her goat — and then at me — and then at her goat again, and so on, alternately —
> — Well, *Maria*, said I softly — What resemblance do you find?

In *Tristram Shandy*, that curious mixture of bawdy comedy and poignant sentiment, Sterne gave expression to what he took to be the paradox of the human condition, at once the stuff of farce and of pathos. Balancing the views of Hobbes and Locke, Shaftesbury and the Latitudinarians, he saw men as both absurd and lovable, enclosed within themselves by the body and the mind, yet capable of being released from that bondage through feeling and the imagination.

Sterne's disturbance of the formal principles of Augustan aesthetics may be seen, then, in part, as the concomitant of a new ontology, defining reality not as the "Art of God," an objective construct designed by the divine Geometrician and providentially controlled, whose unchanging Order may be rationally apprehended, but as the subjective creation of the human understanding, a world fashioned by the mechanism of the mind imposing on a multiplicity of random sensations an order idiosyncratic and, with reference at least to any absolute conception of truth, illusory. As Sterne sensed, the "cosmic syntaxes," to use Earl Wasserman's phrase, had been broken. The world would soon enough no longer seem the well-wrought dramatic Poem of history, inscribed by God's Word with measure, rhyme, and reason, unfolding coherently from Genesis to Apocalypse; it would seem instead the product of the private imagination, responding to the whims of circumstance and the exigencies of desire. Inverting, as it were, the old analogy between macrocosm and microcosm, the individual now defined the structure of his universe. The aimlessness that Swift in *A Tale of a Tub* had presented as the shape of chaos, the projection and embodiment of madness, has become in *Tristram Shandy* the formal expression of a new conception of reality, implying not an aberration from Order, but the imitation of Life.

Not method and reason, the Augustan virtues, but impulse and imagination are the test of truth and the means of communication for Sterne; not symmetry and design, but the "marbled page" is the "motly emblem" of his book. Throughout the novel Tristram mocks the rules that governed Augustan aesthetics, dismissing them as stultifying and irrelevant; for his subject is life, defined not as in other authors by what a man does—he rebukes his readers for their "vile pruriency for fresh adventures in all things"—but by what he *is*, the sum of his "opinions" and feelings. And life in this sense is not to be contained by formal principles (seen now, to use Pope's distinction, as "devised" by officious critics, rather than "discovered" in Nature), by arbitrary aesthetic considerations of unities, of beginnings, middles, and ends, but only by the limitations of mortality: birth and death, the quality of experience and the mechanism of the mind. Unique and individual, the narrative of his life, unlike those of Bunyan's Pilgrim or Tom Jones or Dr. Primrose, is neither allegory nor paradigm nor analogue, for it "stands" for nothing beyond itself. Since Tristram's story is coextensive with himself, it begins, properly, with the night of his begetting; he will trace "every thing in it, as *Horace* says, *ab Ovo*." He is aware that Horace on formal grounds commended Homer for *not* beginning the *Iliad* with the birth of Helen from Leda's egg, but, he insists, "in writing what I have set about, I shall confine myself neither to his rules, nor to any man's rules that ever lived." In *Tristram Shandy*, indeed, the only advocate of the rules of art is Slawkenbergius, whose prodigious tale, with "all the essential and integrant parts" of a Sophoclean drama "rightly disposed" in "the order *Aristotle* first planted them," progresses methodically through "*Protasis, Epistasis, Catastasis*" to its "*Catastrophe* or *Peripeitia*."

Tristram's book, on the contrary, has no more structure than the vagaries of his mind. He pleads, disingenuously and of course in vain, for assistance from those shaping "*Powers*" of Augustan art,

> — which enable mortal man to tell a story worth the hearing, —
> that kindly shew him, where he is to begin it, — and where
> he is to end it, — what he is to put into it, — and what he is
> to leave out, — how much of it he is to cast into shade, — and
> whereabouts he is to throw his light!

If the powers of art haven't abandoned him altogether, their visitations are infrequent and felt in peculiarly Shandean ways: at one point in his narrative, in order to achieve his own version of the Augustan ideal of harmony and proportion, he tears out of his book a particularly fine chapter that threatens to disturb the monotony of his style, thereby ingeniously preserving "that necessary equipoise and balance, (whether of good or bad) betwixt chapter and chapter, from whence the just proportions and harmony of the whole work results." Indeed, in deference to divines and philosophers, cabbage planters and mathematicians, he will try, he assures us, to bring the divagations of his narrative under control and "to go on with my uncle *Toby's* story, and my own, in a tolerable straight line," aspiring to

the excellency of going on even thus;

---

which is a line drawn as straight as I could draw it, by a writing-master's ruler, (borrowed for that purpose) turning neither to the right hand or to the left.

But Tristram's method, if crazy and capricious by Augustan standards of regularity and symmetry, is faithful enough as a mirror of the fluid, shifting processes of the mind, working by impulse and association. It is even, as he facetiously remarks, "the most religious" method, "for I begin with writing the first sentence — and trusting to Almighty God for the second." What matters in *Tristram Shandy* is not pattern, but the flow of soul, the registering of sensation and the movement of thought. As a man of sensibility, Tristram would revise Descartes's essential premiss: "I think, *and* feel, and therefore I am." His procedures as an author reflect a new conception of the doctrine of mimesis, of the way in which form recapitulates ontology. Taking a pair of chapters to record the conversation between Walter and Toby as they descend the stairs, he warns that since they are "in a talking humour," there may be as many chapters as steps:

— let that be as it will, Sir, I can no more help it than my destiny: — A sudden impulse comes across me — drop the curtain, *Shandy* — I drop it — Strike a line here across the paper, *Tristram* — I strike it — and hey for a new chapter?

The duce of any other rule have I to govern myself by in this affair — and if I had one — as I do all things out of all rule — I would twist it and tear it to pieces, and throw it into the fire when I had done — Am I warm? I am, and the cause demands it — a pretty story! is a man to follow rules — or rules to follow him?

Sterne rejects the rationalist aesthetic of the Augustans for fancy and free form, imitating not Nature's geometry — what the critics and theologians of the preceding hundred years had seen as her fondness for regularity and symmetry — but her profusion, caprice, and infinite variety. It is the "variety" his perpetual digressions provide that is "the sunshine . . . the life, the soul of reading," banishing cold winter. Sterne's metaphors for his book suggest Nature's vitality, not her intricate design; freedom, organicism are his aim.

If authors and gardeners may be compared, he will plant no cabbages "one by one, in straight lines, and stoical distances"; he is of a party with Launcelot Brown and Humphry Repton, preferring to express in art Nature's wildness and abhorrence of constraint, where at "every step that's taken, the judgment is surprised by the imagination." He is least of all a builder of Palladian structures:

> And what of this new book the whole world makes such a rout about? — Oh! 'tis out of all plumb, my Lord, — quite an irregular thing! — not one of the angles at the four corners was a right angle. — I had my rule and compasses, &c. my Lord, in my pocket. — Excellent critic!

Instead of such readers, give him "that man whose generous heart will give up the reins of his imagination into his author's hands, — be pleased he knows not why, and cares not wherefore." Give him humour and a spark of genius, "and send *Mercury*, with the *rules and compasses*, if he can be spared, with my compliments to — ."

But the form of *Tristram Shandy* is a more remarkable development than these explanations would suggest. If from one point of view it represents a new conception of how Nature ought to be imitated in a work of art — by impulse rather than by rule — from another point of view it is not so much a celebration of freedom as a protest against the limitations of the human condition. Behind Sterne's bawdy games and verbal antics one may sense a troubled awareness of man's transiency, impotence, and isolation — the irreducible facts of life which his book is designed to oppose and mitigate, not only by turning them to laughter, but by transmuting them into another substance more lasting, vital, mutual: the substance of his art.

Tristram's book, as we remarked earlier, is an attempt to master and make permanent that most fugitive and puzzling thing, his life. It is the objectification, the palpable projection and embodiment, of his subjective self. His writing, he implies, bears the same relation to his life as the body to the mind, and "exactly like a jerkin, and a jerkin's lining" the two are inseparable and coextensive; living and writing, he assures us, are "in my case . . . the same thing." His book, he hopes, will contain and encompass him, excluding "nothing which has touched me," and by it, therefore, he will know himself and be known to others, a relationship that will "grow into familiarity" and "terminate in friendship." He intends to write and publish two volumes of his "life" every year for as long as he lives, which procedure — thanks to the digressive-progressive "machinery" of his work sustaining it, as the world itself is sustained, by the reconciliation of "two contrary motions"—he trusts will keep it "a-going these forty years, if it pleases the fountain of health to bless me so long with life and good spirits." Our sense of the identity of Tristram's life and his book is reinforced by his frequent references to the precise moment and place of composition, inviting us to imagine him in the actual process of writing, which, as he constantly insists, is identical with the processes of his thought and feeling. One consequence of this pretence, in fact, is that his book has become more real to him than his life, providing him with a knowable, even a tangible, identity and serving as a compensation for mortality. Whereas Tristram is the sport of Fortune, frustrated by circumstances, impotent, dying of consumption, his *Life and Opinions* will, he trusts, enjoy a better fate and "shall make its way in the world, much better than its master has done before it——." Though, as Wayne Booth has argued, Sterne may not have intended to continue his novel beyond the ninth volume, it is clear that the illusion he wished to enforce is that the book is open ended; for from Tristram's point of view, life itself must end with the final sentence.

Tristram's attempt to make his book contain him must of course fail, for, by his own calculation, he is living "364 times faster" than he can write; "I shall," he laments, "never overtake myself." As an author he shares his father's fate, who scribbles away at his *Tristrapœdia* while "every day a page or two became of no consequence." As we are aware from the first chapter, Time—the clock and all it implies of frustration and mortality—is the marplot of Tristram's life and art. If his book offers him the hope of permanence, of objectifying and fixing the flow of consciousness, the hopelessness of his efforts as an author to "overtake" himself heightens our sense of the limitations of the human condition and, most especially, of the inevitability of death. If Time is always leaving him behind, Mortality is at his back, "that death-looking, long-striding scoundrel of a scare-sinner, who is posting after me." The finality of death—Yorick's, Bobby's, the threat of Tristram's own—is one of the less cheerful aspects of the Shandean world, rendered by that memorial to utter darkness and annihilation, the black pages, and by "the mortality of *Trim's* hat," which brings its meaning home even to Susannah:

> ——"Are we not here now,"——continued the corporal, "and are we not"——(dropping his hat plumb upon the ground——and pausing, before he pronounced the word)——"gone! in a moment?" The descent of the hat was as if a heavy lump of clay had been kneaded into the crown of it.——Nothing could have expressed the sentiment of mortality, of which it was the type and forerunner, like it,——his hand seemed to vanish from under it,——it

fell dead, — the corporal's eye fix'd upon it, as upon a corps, — and *Susannah* burst into a flood of tears.

As far as the novel would allow — which is, like life, a temporal mode whose effects must be achieved through the arrangement of words in sequence — Sterne's objective in *Tristram Shandy* was to develop a form that would release us from the bondage of Time. He attempts by various devices to stop the clock, by which previous narratives had been regulated — *Tom Jones*, for example, whose every book carries a signature of the years or weeks or days in which the action transpires. Sterne instead leads us into the timeless regions of the consciousness where past and present are one and simultaneously apprehended: "for in good truth, when a man is telling a story in the strange way I do mine, he is obliged continually to be going backwards and forwards to keep all tight together in the reader's fancy." The illusion of simultaneity is for the most part achieved by Sterne's digressive technique; the movement "backwards and forwards" by impulse and the association of ideas, enforcing the distinction which Walter found in Locke between chronological and psychological time, the one ticking out our physical existence, the other dependent upon the succession of ideas in the mind, by which "*we know that we do exist.*" In this manner Tristram, fleeing from Death across France, may escape the limitations of time and space:

> — Now this is the most puzzled skein of all — for in this last chapter, as far at least as it has help'd me through *Auxerre*, I have been getting forwards in two different journies together, and with the same dash of the pen — for I have got entirely out of *Auxerre* in this journey which I am writing now, and am got half way out of *Auxerre* in that which I shall write hereafter — There is but a certain degree of perfection in every thing; and by pushing at something beyond that, I have brought myself into such a situation, as no traveller ever stood before me; for I am this moment walking across the market-place of *Auxerre* with my father and my uncle *Toby*, in our way back to dinner — and I am this moment also entering *Lyons* with my post-chaise broke into a thousand pieces — and I am moreover this moment in a handsome pavillion built by *Pringello*, upon the banks of the *Garonne*, which Mons. *Sligniac* has lent me, and where I now sit rhapsodizing all these affairs.

In the attempt to suggest the simultaneity of time past and time present in the consciousness, Sterne anticipates, however crudely, certain experimental novelists of our own century. In treating what might be called the physical dimension of his narrative, recording actions which in life must necessarily occur in time, he is no less inventive, achieving an effect analogous to the "stop-action" technique of modern cinematography. In chapter 21 of the first volume, for example, Toby begins to reply to his brother:

> I think, replied my uncle *Toby*, taking his pipe from his mouth, and striking the head of it two or three times upon the nail of his left thumb, as he began his sentence, — I think, says he: —

The description is repeated, and Toby finally allowed to complete the sentence, ten chapters later (2, 6), Tristram having interrupted the narrative for that space in order to fill in his uncle's character, leaving him "all this while . . . knocking the ashes out of his tobacco pipe." Similarly, the account of Walter and Toby descending the stairs is slowed down to the point virtually of suspended animation, as Walter takes a step, draws back his leg, takes the step over again, and the pair are left at last having progressed no farther than the first landing. But the implications of this device in terms of what might be called the "metaphysics" of Sterne's novel are rendered almost paradigmatically in the scene where news of Bobby's death is reported in the kitchen: after Trim drops his hat, the "type" of mortality, Tristram, so to speak, rewinds the reel to play the action over again, slowing it down to analyse its meaning and effect. At such moments, Sterne freezes time, holding an act or gesture indefinitely suspended while allowing the mind to run free. We have the illusion at least that the threat of Time has been neutralized and fugitive experience made permanent.

If Sterne found the theory of duration useful in opposing the tyranny of Time, we have seen that he was less happy about another implication of Locke's epistemology: solipsism. Perhaps the most striking emblem in Sterne's works of this fundamental limitation of the human condition is the image of Yorick at the start of his sentimental journey through alien countries, sitting alone in the stationary *désobligeant*, with blinds drawn against the solicitations of charity, writing his Preface on the difficulties of communication. In *Tristram Shandy* Sterne is no less interested in the problem of our isolation and separateness, of how we may be known to others and in turn know them. Before beginning to draw his uncle Toby from his Hobbyhorse, Tristram regrets that there is no "*Momus*'s glass" to reveal the characters of men, no window in the human breast by which the soul might be viewed "stark naked" and "all her motions, — her machinations" observed. Unfortunately, he reminds us, "our minds shine not through the body, but are wrapt up here in a dark covering of uncrystalized flesh and blood." What Sterne attempts, as it were, is to make his narrative of the Shandys substitute for "*Momus*'s glass," to devise a form by which a printed book might serve to disclose character, through words and images uniting author and reader in a mutual and liberating act of imaginative understanding.

If language traditionally is the medium of rational discourse, through words appealing to the judgement, Sterne had doubts about its efficacy. Like Locke in book 3 of the *Essay*, he regarded words as imprecise and treacherous; refracted through the distorting lens of our preconceptions and prejudices, they tend to inhibit communication and to confirm us in our private systems of self-enclosure. Unlike Locke, he preferred imagination to judgement as the agency of understanding. Though novels must of course be written in words and appeal to the judgements of their readers, Sterne strives to overcome the inherent limitations of the form by deliberately exploiting the ambiguities of language so as to engage the reader's imagination: writing, Tristram remarks,

> when properly managed, (as you may be sure I think mine is) is but a different name for conversation. . . . The truest respect which you can pay to the reader's understanding, is to halve this matter amicably, and leave him something to imagine, in his turn, as well as yourself.
>
> For my own part, I am eternally paying him compliments of this kind, and do all that lies in my power to keep his imagination as busy as my own.

Occasionally, as in the context in which this passage occurs, Sterne eschews words altogether, inviting the reader to "imagine" speeches, descriptions, events. He may even provide him with a blank page, so that he may please his "fancy" by painting the Widow Wadman to his own mind. More often, however, he relies on the ambiguities of language to achieve some of his most distinctive comic effects. Most things in Shandy-land—words not least among them—have, as Walter puts it, "two handles": Toby's references to "curtins and horn-works" provide Dr. Slop with the opportunity for bawdy punning; there is confusion about the meanings of mortars, and bridges, and noses—most especially, noses. For which reason Tristram finds it inexcusable that he should have neglected to define his terms, the obligation of all true philosophers:

> Heaven is witness, how the world has revenged itself upon me for leaving so many openings to equivocal strictures, — and for depending so much as I have done, all along, upon the cleanliness of my reader's imaginations.

> ——Here are two senses, cried *Eugenius*, as we walk'd along, pointing with the fore finger of his right hand to the word *Crevice*, in the fifty-second page of the second volume of this book of books, —— here are two senses, —— quoth he. —— And here are two roads, replied I, turning short upon him, —— a dirty and a clean one, —— which shall we take? —— The clean, —— by all means, replied *Eugenius*. *Eugenius*, said I, stepping before him, and laying my hand upon his breast, —— to define is to distrust.

But Tristram will define, nevertheless — with such scrupulous exactness that we never afterward encounter the word *nose* in his book without applying a phallic interpretation. At other times Sterne's bawdry is the effect of his relying on our imaginations to fill in hiatuses in his text, or to complete syntactical constructions that he has carefully interrupted — a device best remembered from the final abortive sentence of *A Sentimenal Journey*. By such means he breaks down our sense of separateness, implicating the reader in his comedy. If ratiocination multiplies distinctions and confirms us in our solipsism, the imagination — and especially the sexual imagination — reminds us of what we have in common, drawing us out of our "caverns and hiding-places."

A further distinctive feature of Sterne's art is his attempt to find alternatives to language as a means of communication. Since we are creatures "cloathed with bodies, and governed by our imaginations," we are most immediately and powerfully affected not by the abstractions that words imply, but by impressions conveyed directly to the heart by the senses. In this respect, the painter or musician has the advantage over the artist in words, as after Locke eighteenth-century aestheticians such as Jonathan Richardson were well aware:

> Words [Richardson writes] paint to the imagination, but every man forms the thing to himself in his own way: language is very imperfect: there are innumerable colours and figures for which we have no name, and an infinity of other ideas which have no certain words universally agreed upon as denoting them; whereas the painter can convey his ideas of these things clearly, and without ambiguity; and what he says every one understands in the sense he intends it.
>
> And this is a language that is universal; men of all nations hear the poet, moralist, historian, divine or whatever other character the painter assumes, speaking to them in their own mother tongue.
>
> Painting has another advantage over words; and that is, it

pours ideas into our minds, words only drop them. The whole scene opens at one view, whereas the other way lifts up the curtain by little and little.

Sterne, too, saw words in this way, as impeding rather than promoting intercourse between men. In his dispute with Locke over the function and importance of the imagination, Tristram rejects the philosopher's mode of logical discourse in order to argue by analogy, using wit, the synthesizing power of the mind, to prove that wit is equal at least to judgement as a means to understanding:

> I hate set dissertations, — and above all things in the world, 'tis one of the silliest things in one of them, to darken your hypothesis by placing a number of tall, opake words, one before another, in a right line, betwixt your own and your readers conception, — when in all likelihood, if you had looked about, you might have seen something standing, or hanging up, which would have cleared the point at once . . . [— something, for instance, such as the cane chair he is sitting on:] Will you give me leave to illustrate this affair of wit and judgment, by the two knobs on the top of the back of it, — they . . . will place what I have to say in so clear a light, as to let you see through the drift and meaning of my whole preface, as plainly as if every point and particle of it was made up of sun beams.

Seeking new strategies to overcome the inherent limitations of his form, Sterne throughout *Tristram Shandy* prefers to "illustrate" rather than relate, for "the eye . . . has the quickest commerce with the soul, — gives a smarter stroke, and leaves something more inexpressible upon the fancy, than words can either convey — or sometimes get rid of." One celebrated manifestation of this motive in the novel is his occasional abandonment of words altogether in favour of visual devices — the black and marbled pages, the diagrams of his narrative, the squiggle on the page that makes us see Trim's flourish with his stick. Another is his attempt through words to render what recent psychologists have called "body language": those gestures or postures of the body — such as Toby's freeing the fly, or Trim's dropping his hat, or Walter's physical attitude as he lies sprawled upon the bed in sorrow — which express the sentiments of the heart more vividly than speech can do.

> — There are a thousand unnoticed openings, continued my father, which let a penetrating eye at once into a man's soul; and I maintain it, added he, that a man of sense does not lay down his hat

in coming into a room, — or take it up in going out of it, but something escapes, which discovers him.

This deliberate appeal to the senses includes the ear as well as the eye. At the most trivial level, Sterne will use onomatopoetic devices to help us hear a fiddle tuning up, a ditty being hummed, the crack of a coachman's whip. More important are the ways in which the inarticulate sounds his characters utter reveal their feelings as effectively as their physical movements and attitudes. Toby is a notable example: though he is no match for his brother in a debate, he can silence him by whistling a few bars of *Lillabullero*, his "*Argumentum Fistulatorium*"; his "Humph!" grunted in reply to Dr. Slop's account of Romish doctrine serves "as well as if he had wrote a whole volume against the seven sacraments." And Sterne is fully aware of another advantage of the spoken as opposed to the written word, since meaning may be determined by tone of voice. "A fiddlestick!" answers the Widow Wadman in reply to Toby's innocent suggestion that the pleasure of begetting children may be some compensation for the trouble they cause their mothers:

> Now [Tristram observes] there are such an infinitude or notes, tunes, cants, chants, airs, looks, and accents with which the word *fiddlestick* may be pronounced in all such causes as this, every one of 'em impressing a sense and meaning as different from the other, as *dirt* from *cleanliness* — That Casuists (for it is an affair of conscience on that score) reckon up no less than fourteen thousand in which you may do either right or wrong.
>
> Mrs. *Wadman* hit upon the *fiddlestick*, which summoned up all my uncle *Toby*'s modest blood into his cheeks —

Though such strategies contribute to the "oddness" of *Tristram Shandy* as a work of fiction, there is more to them than mere whimsy. As attempts to circumvent the limitations of the novel form, to render scene and character *physically*, they are the expression of Sterne's belief that life must be felt in order to be known, that the way out of the self is through the senses — the eye, the ear, the touch: those organs by which we relate to and interpret the impingent world. There is in his novel as in the story of Toby's Hobbyhorse a sense in which words, though perhaps not quite fatal, perplex the understanding and prevent communication. Like Toby, Tristram attempts to comprehend his world (and to help his reader comprehend it) by objectifying it. By stretching the resources of language so that prose approaches the condition of sensible experience, Sterne makes of his novel a kind of "*Momus*'s glass," disclosing the hearts and souls of his characters. In the sensationalism upon which the new philosophy was based, he found a way of mitigating the solipsism which it implied, a way of reconciling the contradictory views of Locke and the Latitudinarians.

Appealing to the senses and the imagination rather than the judgement, proceeding by impulse rather than design, rejecting chronological structure for the illusion of the flow of consciousness, Sterne represents a revolutionary conception of the ways in which art imitates, in Fielding's phrase, "what really exists." For as the Augustan Age passed into the Age of Sensibility, the object of the artist's imitation was shifting from ideal Nature to the individual consciousness. Despite their resemblances, *A Tale of a Tub* and *Tristram Shandy* violate the formal expectations of their first readers for diametrically different ends. What is in Swift an aberration from the norms of rational order, implying the madness and materialism of the Modern world, has become in Sterne the image of reality. The attitudes of these two writers toward solipsism, imagination, sense, and time serve to define the aesthetic and intellectual contexts of the "Augustan" and the "Modern" modes.

Sterne and the Nostalgia for Reality

Robert Alter

> Tristram Shandy *is the most typical novel of world literature.*
> VIKTOR SHKLOVSKY, *The Theory of Prose*

> *But* Tristram Shandy, *my friend, was made and formed to baffle all criticism.*
> LAURENCE STERNE, *Letters*

One of the characteristic reflexes of the self-conscious novel is to flaunt "naive" narrative devices, rescuing their usability by exposing their contrivance, working them into a highly patterned narration which reminds us that all representations of reality are, necessarily, stylizations. Perhaps the most obvious example is the ostentatious narrator, beginning with Cervantes's mitotic multiplication of narrators and commentators, through to Fielding's urbanely ironic contriver, to the zany jugglers of narrative convention in Sterne and Diderot, and on, most recently, to the composite self-observing narrator of Nabokov's *Ada* and the ventriloquistic "Victorian" voice that reports the action in John Fowles's *The French Lieutenant's Woman*. Another central case in point is the interpolated tale. In *Don Quixote* the device is sometimes used to present fractured or distorted mirror images of the main action, and more pervasively, to provide a series of contrasts in narrative texture, placing against the comic realism of the mock-chivalric novel insets of pastoral, picaresque, exotic romance and adventure, cautionary tales. In mid-eighteenth-century England, where the explicit imitation of Cervantes is most abundantly evident, Fielding puts interpolation to similar use though in a far more symmetrically fashioned narrative design, while Smollett, brilliant backslider in the art of the novel, uses the naive device with untroubled naiveté. Beyond them (in every sense of the preposition), Sterne insists on the ultimate implications, aesthetic,

From *Partial Magic: The Novel as a Self-Conscious Genre.* © 1975 by the Regents of the University of California. University of California Press, 1975.

psychological, and epistemological, of telling stories within stories, being in this as in most other respects the great *jusqu'auboutiste* of the self-conscious novel.

The very notion, of course, of interpolation tends to break down in a book where virtually all progression is digression. The story of Le Fever's death, Slawkenbergius's Tale, Trim's amours, even Tristram's extended flight across Europe, can be felt only minimally as "insets" in a novel where at every turn of a phrase, at every turn of the stairs in Shandy Hall, the mind goes skittering off in self-delighting demonstration of its own essential waywardness. The general effect of all this is a highly polarized version of the paradox of evident artifice as seeming reality. The zigzag movement of narration is an authentic rendering of the mind's own resistance to the neatness of pattern and schematization, and at the same time it is a continuous declaration by the author of the artful arbitrariness of all authorial decisions—as his graphic introduction of actual zigzags and convoluted lines (6, 40) suggests. But to see how radical Sterne is in the practice of fictional self-consciousness, it is worth looking closely at one of his interpolations within a digression. In volume 7, as Tristram leaves the much-interrupted account of his conception, birth, and upbringing to tell the story of his pursuit of health through France and Italy, he pauses over one of the tourist attractions of Lyons, the Tomb of the Two Lovers. This gives him occasion to recount what is purportedly the Tale of the Two Lovers (chap. 31):

> O! There is a sweet aera in the life of man, when, (the brain being tender and fibrillous, and more like pap than any thing else)—
> a story read of two fond lovers, separated from each other by cruel parents, and by still more cruel destiny—
>> *Amandus* — He
>> *Amanda* — She —
> each ignorant of the other's course,
>> He — east
>> She — west
> *Amandus* taken captive by the *Turks*, and carried to the emperor of *Morocco's* court, where the princess of *Morocco* falling in love with him, keeps him twenty years in prison, for the love of his *Amanda.* —
>> She — (*Amanda*) all the time wandering barefoot, and with dishevell'd hair, o'er rocks and mountains enquiring for *Amandus*
> — *Amandus! Amandus!* — making every hill and vally to echo back his name —
>> *Amandus! Amandus!*

at every town and city sitting down forlorn at the gate——Has *Amandus*!——has my *Amandus* enter'd?——till, going round, and round, and round the world——chance unexpected bringing them at the same moment of the night, though by different ways, to the gate of *Lyons* their native city, and each in well known accents calling out aloud,

Is *Amandus* ⎫
Is my *Amanda* ⎭ still alive?

they fly into each others arms, and both drop down dead for joy.

There is a soft aera in every gentle mortal's life, where such a story affords more *pabulum* to the brain, than all the *Frusts*, and *Crusts*, and *Rusts* of antiquity, which travellers can cook up for it.

We have had occasion to observe how Cervantes's hero weaves a reflexive, ambiguously luminous poetry out of literary clichés. This passage from Sterne is, like many of Don Quixote's speeches, a tissue of patient clichés, but a different principle of parody is at work here, the effect of which is much more severely reductionist. In regard to details of plot, such as they are, the story of the two lovers could easily serve as one of the interpolated tales in *Don Quixote*, including as it does a separation of fond lovers by cruel parents, a captivity in Morocco, a Moorish princess in love with her Christian slave, and a final tragically ecstatic reunion. What Sterne does, however, with these elements is to distill from them a quintessential scheme of all such tales of romance, the conspicuousness of the scheme precluding any illusion of reality. In all his cap-and-bells antics, Sterne is one of the shrewdest literary critics of his century, and a central insight of his novel is that any literary convention means a schematization—and thus a misrepresentation—of reality. *Tristram Shandy* abundantly illustrates, moreover, that a new "authentic" literature liberated from conventions is a sheer impossibility. The act of literary communication can take place only by virtue of certain tacit contractual agreements between writer and reader—about the meaning and nature of words, about typography and pagination, about chapter divisions, about characterization and motivation, about cause and effect in narration, and much more. Whatever Sterne's commitment to spontaneity, he knows that the attempt to transcend these conventional agreements would reduce the literary feast (Fielding's favored metaphor) to mere word salad, and so instead he makes us continually conscious of the conventions, exploring their limits, their implicit falsity, their paradoxical power to transmit fractional truths of experience. Sterne treats each literary convention much as the inquisitive lady in Slawkenbergius's second tale (9, 21) treats a certain unmentioned something—"looks at it——considers it——samples it——measures it——

stretches it — wets it — dries it — then takes . . . teeth both to the warp and weft of it."

Imaginative play with the duplicity of literary conventions is by no means the invention of the novel — one has only to think of the toying with supposed source-manuscripts in medieval romance and the use of inductions and plays-within-plays in Renaissance theater. There is considerable justice in Roland Barthes's lapidary formulation of the issue, though the attractions of aphoristic neatness may lead him to a degree of overstatement: "To give the imaginary the formal guarantee of the real, while leaving this sign the ambiguity of a double object, at once verisimilar and false, is a constant operation in all Western art." What the novel, specifically, has been able to do, as the post-Gutenberg genre generally designed to be enjoyed by each reader in privacy at his own tempo with leisure to reread and freedom to skip, is to explore the ambiguity of its imaginary "signs" in slow motion, microscopically, from multiple angles, and, if the writer chooses, quite relentlessly. *Tristram Shandy* is in fact "the most typical novel of world literature" in this one peculiar sense, that it represents an extreme realization of an underlying direction implicit in the novel-form and followed out elsewhere less rigorously or less spectacularly by other novelists. If Barthes, taking his metaphor from the theater, can assert that "in the West . . . there is no art that does not point a finger to its own mask," one must say that the distinctive situation of the novel enables the performer (for every narrator is that, none more conspicuously than Tristram) to step down from the stage, walk among the audience, invite the individual spectators to examine his mask, consider its substance, design, texture, weight, coloring, even guess about the reality of the face behind the mask.

The Tale of the Two Lovers illustrate how merciless this examination can become. It is, quite deliberately, the reduction of a tale of romance to an embarrassingly bare outline. The outline quality of the narration is felt not only in the succinct catalogue of formulaic phrases — "separated . . . by cruel parents, and by still more cruel destiny," "wandering barefoot, and with dishevell'd hair," "each in well known accents calling," et cetera — but in the typography as well. First we have the exposition of the story in four words, two lines, set at the center of the page, the lovers in perfect symmetrical parallel, separated from each other by a line space and distinguished from one another by a Latin gender-ending ("*Amandus* — He / *Amanda* — She — "). The designation of the lovers merely by the gerundive forms that mean "he who is to be loved" and "she who is to be loved" is an ultimate reduction of Cervantes's ambiguous play with the magic of naming names. If the coinage "Rocinante" points a finger to the mask, the names "Amandus" and "Amanda" turn the mask into a perfect transparency. (Significantly, the one central attempt at name-magic made by a character in the novel is deflected by circumstance, Walter's wished for "Trismegistus"—thricepowerful—truncated to "Tristram," a sorry creature indeed.) After the exposition, in another indentation, we are given the complication of the plot, again in a strictly schematic parallelism of four words ("He—east / She—west"). Finally, once more at the center of the page, we get the requisite recognition scene, the ever-parallel lovers, though still a line space apart, now at last united by the gently curving embrace of a typographical bracket. This is followed by a denouement of thirteen swift words (fifteen syllables) which conclude in an iambic cadence on "joy." To cap the story, Tristram, adhering to the niceties of a rondo form, offers at the end an incremental repetition of his initial sentence, calling our attention to the purely verbal medium of the storytelling by the italicized, capitalized rhyme words, *Frusts* (apparently Sterne's own coinage from the Latin *frustum*), *Crusts*, and *Rusts*.

The entire "reality" of the tale, then, is a compound of rigidly formulaic devices conveyed to us on the printed page through the mechanics of typography. The final turn, however, of the reductionist screw is made here not through the schematizing parody itself but through the parenthetical commentary at the beginning together with its concluding echo at the end. The era in a man's life when he relishes such stories is "sweet" and "soft"—like pabulum—which is just the consistency of the story itself or of any brain that would take a liking to it. Sterne's rapid movement from the realm of feeling to the realm of material processes is especially worth noting because it reflects an impelling problematic consciousness in *Tristram Shandy*. The tale begins with "sweet," a sensory word used figuratively. From there we proceed at once to a "tender" brain and are misled for a brief instant to read the adjective as an item in the vocabulary of sentimentalism before we see that it is followed by a medical term, "fibrillous," which in turn leads into the slap-in-the-face comparison, "like pap." Tenderness, then, is a purely physical condition of semiliquid gray matter, and we are invited to infer that all such fine structures of sentiment issue from some physical substratum which may be less than edifying to contemplate.

In the world of *Tristram Shandy*, as at least two of Sterne's more perceptive critics have recently noted, there is a constant dynamic tension between the mental and the material spheres. Extravagant attention is devoted to the minute rendering of each—to Corporal Trim's desolation over his brother's plight, on the one hand, and to the elaborate series of movements that produce the puffing of a pipe, on the other hand. The contiguity of the two realms is evident, their interconnection and causal relation a continual enigma, a continual source of frustration, comedy, and surprise. If one wonders why Sterne should be so much more ruthless as a critic of literary artifice than Cervantes, a chief reason would have to be that he writes at a point in intellectual history—for his novel is eminently a document of intellectual history—when there was manifest cause for worry that the tender feelings evoked by the refinements of literature might be finally just a question of mushy gray matter.

Tristram Shandy was created toward the end of the great century of confident mechanistic science that began with the publication of Newton's *Principia* in 1687. Descartes's metaphysical analysis had introduced an ontological cleavage between mental and material existence that would remain a crux of philosophical debate for generations to come. In the realm of physics pure and simple, Newton founded an explanation of the physical world on what seemed to be an entirely adequate basis of measurement, with quantification in terms of mass held as the key. Conscious of the new Newtonian physics, Locke transferred the mechanistic mode of explanation to the realm of psychology. Existence was split into "primary qualities," which were wholly quantifiable, and "secondary qualities," projected onto objects by the mind. The world of value and sensuous opulence was reduced to a mental construct; nature in and of itself was colorless, tasteless, odorless, and, finally, senseless. Lockean psychology, with its mechanistic model of the *tabula rasa* and the association of ideas, is a preeminent instance of what Whitehead has characterized as the Fallacy of Misplaced Concreteness.

It is no wonder that Sterne begins his novel by throwing a machine into the Lockean system, that regularly wound clock linked in poor Mrs. Shandy's mind with her husband's monthly conjugal performances "from an unhappy association of ideas which have no connection in nature" (1, 4). If Locke, as the regnant figure of philosophical psychology for Sterne's century, provided a basis for the associative method of *Tristram Shandy*, the novel treats him even more as a teacher to be taunted, a hobgoblin to be exorcised, because his ontological devaluation of the imagination and its products cuts the ground from under the whole enterprise of literature. *Tristram Shandy* is a continuous demonstration and celebration of the irrepressible power and ubiquity of the imagination, but at the same time Sterne must repeatedly concede the possibility, so palpable in the thought of his age, that the imagination is a cheat, a purveyor of substanceless flim-flam in a mechanistically determined physical universe. Martin Price, with the problem of philosophical dualism particularly in mind, has aptly caught the tenor of this tension in Sterne's novel between two opposed but somehow contiguous realms:

Sterne carries the duality of man to its ultimate expression. He comically exaggerates the outside view of man as a physically determined creature, the sport of chance or mechanical causation, the lonely product of a valueless material world. He exaggerates no less the inside view of man as a creature of feeling, convinced phenomenologically that he has a soul, creating the world in which he chiefly lives by the energy of his own imagination. The disjunction is as violent as Pascal's.

What sharpens the paradoxicality of Sterne's fiction is the fact that the recent development of the novel as a genre has made available striking techniques of comic and serious realism at the very moment when the new science and philosophy were raising questions about the inherent connection between imaginative literature and reality. Parody, together with direct imitation and plain borrowing, is pervasive in *Tristram Shandy*, Sterne's models including Rabelais, Montaigne, Burton, Descartes, Locke, Swift, and a host of lesser writers, scholastic, scientific, historical, and satirical. It is worth noting in particular, however, the way he parodies all the principal models of novel writing available to him by pushing the method of each to its logical extreme. Written scarcely twenty years after the form had got fully under way in England, *Tristram Shandy* is the first novel about the crisis of the novel.

"Cervantick" realism, Sterne perceived, operates by a repeated juxtaposition of soaring fantasy with earth-bound, coarse-grained actuality, the quixotic principle colliding with the sanchesque. *Tristram Shandy* comically and philosophically expands this central strategy of *Don Quixote* by making it the ubiquitous pattern of every man's relation to every other and to the world of physical existence. The obvious Quixote-Sancho pairings in the novel, Toby and Trim, Walter and Mrs. Shandy, in fact suggest an infinite *dédoublement,* for everyone is quixotic in putting some private construction of the mind — some personal lexicon — upon reality, and any other is a potential Sancho to one's own quixotry: Walter to Toby and Toby to Walter, Jenny to Tristram, Obadiah (and his horse) to Dr. Slop, the scullion to Trim, the bull to all the Shandys. One functional justification for the pervasiveness of double entente in the novel is that sexuality is conceived as every person's Sancho Panza — the hot chestnut in the codpiece, "that one thing which *Dolly's* hand is in search of" (2, 2), the universal human preoccupation that binds us while systems sizzle, hypotheses hatch, and ratiocination goes its merry solipsistic way.

From Fielding, himself the author of a novel "Written," as its title page proclaimed, "in Imitation of the *Manner* of Cervantes," Sterne adopted the self-conscious, self-advertising narrator who reflects discursively on the innovative nature of his fiction as he makes it. Here, again, it is Sterne's peculiar brilliance as a borrower to push so far what he has taken that it is no longer a device or a technique but a fundamental problematic, both literary and philosophical. The narrators of *Joseph Andrews* and *Tom Jones* call attention to themselves as artificers in a variety of ingenious and elegantly ironic ways. The narrator of *Tristram Shandy* draws us so intimately and inventively into the present tense of his writing that all the other elaborately indicated times of narrated events ultimately dissolve into it, and the stumbling chase of a self trying to catch its own or any experience through an act of written communication becomes the true plot of the novel.

The contradictory fusion of conjuration and critique is at its most spectacular in this novel, typicality attained over and over through extremeness. We know, on the one hand, that the clowning narrator is less a personage than a pretext, a mask for the Laurence Sterne who, to pick up one of several such notations he offers us, pens the eighteenth chapter of the first volume in his Yorkshire study on March 9, 1759. All the talk in *Tristram* about critics and different kinds of readers, about time, duration, and narrative conventions, the black and blank and marbled pages that force us to see the process of semantic integration through which each reader assembles the world of a novel in his head—all these make us aware of novel writing as a highly complicated activity of construction with the materials of convention. Yet Tristram, precisely because the distance between him and Sterne flickers and fades, also seems very real without novelistic realization, humanly poignant in his urgency to get something of himself across to us through the labyrinth of literary and linguistic conventions that surrounds him, that surrounds all of us. At one remove of creation from Tristram, we are intermittently moved to assent to the reality of the personages—Sterne's inventions—that populate his story because we identify with him in his effort to make his experience real through writing. Fielding's Squire Western remains a manifest fabrication, brilliantly lifelike, wonderfully memorable, but clearly a device in an invented narrative manipulated by the novelist's narrating persona. Sterne's Uncle Toby we know is a fabrication as well, but at times, by virtue of this peculiar novel's mirror game of mimesis, he seems to be something more: because Tristram is his own elusive subject, we want Tristram's tale of his uncle to be real so that Tristram can be real, we want to accept as facts of experience the minute rendering of Toby's sorrow over the death of the fly, Toby's childlike joy over his model fortifications, his terror of Woman on the sofa next to the Widow Wadman. It is not really so surprising that generations of readers unattuned to Sterne's sophistication as a self-conscious novelist and out of sympathy with the slippery play of his sexual wit were never-

theless able to enjoy the novel sentimentally for the touching lifelike eccentricities of its characters.

Sterne's radical transformation of the self-conscious narrator, which he
picked up from Fielding, is perhaps most suggestively revealed in the role
death comes to play in *Tristram Shandy*. Fielding's self-conscious narrator by
his very nature implies comedy of a particularly pure kind: the narrated action, we are continually reminded, is part of a cunning design where one
assumes the creator will protect the deserving among his creatures from any
real disaster. Death is a narrative convenience through which characters like
Captain Blifil and Tom's father can be eliminated for the purposes of the
plot, but the gallows that cast their shadow over Tom we recognize as an
elaborate authorial joke, the novelist toying with mock-tragedy before he
reveals his comic denouement. In the end, the hero must return to the sunlit
sphere of Paradise Hall where, in the last unfolding vista of married bliss
and propagation, one finds it hard to imagine there has been any First Disobe-
dience that could bring death or woe into this world.

The comedy of *Tristram Shandy* is clearly of another order — not the affirmation of artifice as a means of constructing models of harmonious integration but the use of laughter as the defense action of an embattled psyche,
its chief means of confronting the terrors of loneliness, frustration, pain, of
its own inevitable extinction. There is nothing of Fielding's comic confidence
in the language Sterne chooses to describe his enterprise in his dedicatory
epistle to Pitt: ". . . I live in a constant endeavour to fence against the infir-
mities of ill health, and other evils of life, by mirth; being firmly persuaded
that every time a man smiles, — but much more so, when he laughs, that
it adds something to this Fragment of Life." Sterne's novel begins with the
act of conception that is supposed to lead to the birth of the hero, but a
death — Yorick's — is the most prominent event of the first volume. The famous
black page, prefaced by the double quotation of "Alas, poor YORICK!" reduces
death to a literary and typographical joke, yet paradoxically confronts us with
death as an ultimate, irreducible fact, the final opaqueness beyond the scope
of language and narrative invention, beyond even the tracery of significant
black lines on the white ground of a printed page. Similarly ambiguous attention is lavished on the deaths of Le Fever and Bobby, the element of pathos
being stressed in the former, the hilarious comic discrepancy between event
and response emphasized in the latter case. By the time Death himself knocks
at the door at the beginning of volume 7, mortality is no fictional plaything
but the real motor force that drives Tristram-Sterne on his wild scramble
to write, and write still more. The "vile cough" that wracks Tristram is
autobiographically Sterne's, and death now can no longer be conjured with

but must be eluded—physically, by the flight across Europe, narratively, by devoting digressive attention to anything else the mind can play with, especially anything like codpieces and slit petticoats, because they speak of life. Sterne's nervous yet exuberant bandying with real and imagined death is the clearest illustration of how his extravagantly artifical comic novel opens into an existential realism beyond the purview of comedy, where artifice and artificer collapse into a vulnerable man trying to add something to his Fragment of Life.

This ultimacy of parodistic extrapolation that we have observed in Sterne's relation to Cervantes and Fielding is also detectable in the use to which he puts the other two novelists who were immediate models for him, Smollett and Richardson. In regard to Smollett, of course, the borrowing is more obvious and direct, the humorist's fascination with outrageous eccentricity that links Sterne with the Scottish novelist even leading him to take Commodore Hawser Trunnion's nautical household in *Peregrine Pickle* as a model for Uncle Toby's garden fortifications. Nevertheless, Sterne's imagination of eccentricity and its implications differs profoundly from Smollett's. The Hawser Trunnions and Tom Bowlings and Matthew Brambles that vivify Smollett's fiction are all seen from the safe vantage point of a reasonable, "normal" observer, and so are held at a distance as endearing objects of amusement that entertain through their bizarreness, their wild deviation from an implicit rational norm. In *Tristram Shandy* there are no straight men and there is no norm. The world is entirely peopled with Smollettian eccentrics, rendered, however, in most instances with gentle sympathy. Bizarreness is grasped as an essential condition of every human being living inside his own peculiar skin and peering out on the world through the weirdly refracting medium of his own conceptions and predispositions. Comic eccentricity, then, implies for Sterne the problem of the dysfunction of language that is at the heart of *Tristram Shandy*. Smollett had happily conceived the idea of a series of eccentrics each insisting on his own special vocabulary. Sterne's genius leads him to transmute the phenomenon of private vocabularies into a whole world of mutual misapprehensions and slapstick intersections where communication can take place only (and occasionally) through gesture and intuition, or through the sexuality common to all.

As for Richardson, Sterne may have drawn some inspiration from him for his own interest in the novelistic rendering of sentiment, as some of the literary handbooks claim, but I think what arrested his imagination more decisively in Richardson was the attempt at an exhaustive presentation of reality with the concomitant slowing down of narrative tempo. In Richardson's novels, one feels the palpable weight of minute-by-minute experience conveyed with a particularity of social, psychological, at times even physical detail that is quite new in European fiction. The idea of exhaustive presentation through slow-motion narration intrigued Sterne: the possibilities of its comic exaggeration titillated him; but above all it suggested to him a fundamental problematic bearing on the inherent limitations of literary mimesis. Walter Shandy's advancing foot, hovering over the first step from the landing for the whole length of a chapter in which Sterne reflects upon chapters (4, 10–12), is surely, among other things, a comic blow-up of Richardsonian narrative pace. Here, as elsewhere in the treatment of his novelistic predecessors, the effect of Sterne's parody is not reduction but fantastic expansion, raising over and over the question whether language, with its serial nature and its drastically selective bias, can ever yield an exhaustive account either of a narrated event or of the contents at a particular moment of the narrator's mind. The fantastic character of this expansion is worth stressing because Sterne's ingenious procedures act, like the slow-motion camera, close-ups, odd camera angles, and rapid cutting of different shots in film, to uncover a world of fantastic proportions and connections in the most familiar and prosaic scenes. One sees the aptness of Jean-Jacques Mayoux's characterization of this strange mode of fiction, in his brilliant essay on Sterne, as an "absurd and alienating realism." But the role of fantasy in Sterne's artifice of exaggerated realism is a subject to which we shall return.

We began with a reductionist parody of a tale of romance, the method illustrating how literary convention can be a schematic betrayal of experience, which is multi-faceted, quirky, entrammeled in physical existence. The counterpoint of such parody is the affirmation of an antithetical realism, and what Sterne concentrates on in the last two volumes of *Tristram Shandy*, following upon the parodistic outline of the Tale of Two Lovers in volume 7, is a Shandean transmogrification of the tale of romance that offers one of his many asymptotic approaches to reality. The model here is Trim's amour with the fair Beguine (8, 23), the episode that arrested Diderot's attention enough for him to translate it whole into the ending of *Jacques the Fatalist and His Master*. Like so many of the stories within stories in *Tristram Shandy*, this is a tale told to a misapprehending audience, demonstrating still again how most of us fail to get straight even straight-forward accounts of lived experience because we interpose our own preconceptions and psychological reticences, our own expectations of narrative convention. Trim's tale, quite clearly, is of skilled female fingers on a slow march to an erogenous objective, but the tenderhearted, pap-brained Toby can extract from it only fine literary sentiments:

> The more she rubb'd, and the longer strokes she took — the more
> the fire kindled in my veins — till at length, by two or three

strokes longer than the rest — my passion rose to the highest
pitch — I seized her hand —

— And then, thou clapped'st it to thy lips, *Trim*, said my uncle *Toby* — and madest a speech.

Whether the corporal's amour terminated precisely in the way
my uncle *Toby* described it, is not material; it is enough that it
contain'd in it the essence of all the love-romances which ever
have been wrote since the beginning of the world.

One major impulse of Sterne's realism is to bring etherealizing fancy
and abstracting reason solidly down into the physical realm where, necessarily,
they have their origins. His sexual puns effect this linguistically by constantly reminding us how metaphorical usage develops from a base of physical
experience, whether consciously or not. Thus, in Trim's story, the conventional figure of rising to a high pitch of passion becomes an allusion to the
functioning of erectile tissue, and "passion" has a plain physiological meaning. Trim's dalliance with the Beguine contains the essence of all love romances
ever written because it leads our attention back to the sexual interaction that
is always present in a love story, however the pretensions of the story and
its conventions may try to avoid, disguise, or cosmetize the underlying sexual facts.

Sterne underscores the paradigmatic role of Trim's amour by providing
three different doublings of it in the final volume of the novel. The story
of the romance between Trim's brother Tom and the Jew's widow in the
Lisbon sausage shop is, in the transparent double entente that runs through
the whole chapter (9, 7), another tale of a deft woman's hand stroking "forced
meat," with the good widow finally capitulating when she sees that Tom's
sausage "had more gristle on it." Less messily, Trim's courtship of Bridget
(9, 28) is again a matter of a strategic laying on of hands: "It was somewhat
unfortunate for Mrs. *Bridget*, that she had begun the attack with her manual
exercise, for the Corporal instantly — " at which point the narrative explodes
into three and a half lines of asterisks, leaving us with another variation on
the essence of all love-romances. Bridget's manual attack, in turn, mirrors
in accomplished fact the blushing, hesitant intention of her mistress, the
Widow Wadman, to place her finger over the very place where poor Toby
was wounded at Namur (9, 20).

Now, with this insistence on Trim's tactile affair with the Beguine as
paradigm, it may seem that what passes for realism in Sterne is sexually reductionist. This is not strictly true, however, because Sterne, probably more
than any other writer before Freud, had a conscious awareness of repression
and its manifold implications, the keenness of his comic realism often largely

generated by his shrewd rendering of those implications. The essence of all love romances is not just a male member and female touch but the psychological strategies of coping with those two basic facts by the potential lovers and by the audience. Depending on their various habits of sublimation, avoidance, ambivalent vacillation, impulses to gratification, Shandean lovers are likely to stand under an overarching question mark of misunderstanding, and the reader's personal familiarity with the same sort of habits makes double entente the most appropriate vehicle for the Shandean love romance.

The culminating misunderstanding between Uncle Toby and the Widow Wadman is a vivid case in point. Significantly, Sterne concludes the slow preparation to this climax that has been winding through a volume and a half by one of his most ostentatious overturnings of the conventions of reading and printing. After Tristram has at last invited us to follow Toby and Trim across the Wadman threshold, he introduces two blank pages, labeled "CHAP. XVIII" and "CHAP. XIX" (we will get the chapters out of order ten pages later), and then the twentieth chapter, which begins with two whole paragraphs of asterisks, followed by Toby's mistaken offer to let the widow see the very place where he was wounded. The missing chapters and the asterisks of course heighten comic suspense while reminding us how arbitrary all narrative selections and divisions are. More to our present point, though, this strategic abandoning of language for blank space and printer's symbols is Sterne's visible means of "halving" things, as he says elsewhere, with the reader, "do[ing] all that lies in my power to keep his imagination as busy as my own" (2, 11). Art here points not only to its mask but to its inherent limits, inviting the reader to conjure up for himself the details of a narrative event that in its excitements and emotional complications, its psychological multiplicity, must remain beyond the highly selective reach of language and narration.

After this eloquent use of typographical silences, Sterne returns to language with virtuoso skill. First, Toby makes his generous offer, impervious through his habitual sublimation in siege works to what is obviously uppermost in the mind of this widow who has been waiting so long to be wadded by a man. Her own response to what she misconceives as an offer to get to the naked essence of love romance is brilliantly rendered by Sterne:

Mrs. *Wadman* blush'd——look'd towards the door——turn'd pale——blush'd slightly again——recovered her natural colour—— blushed worse than ever; which for the sake of the unlearned reader, I translate thus——

"L——d! *I cannot look at it——*
What would the world say if I look'd at it?
I should drop down, if I look'd at it——

> *I wish I could look at it —*
> *There can be no sin in looking at it.*
> *— I will look at it."*

Sterne's use of stacatto pauses and dashes achieves the precision of a quasi-musical notation of minute gesture — here, the quick ebb and flow of color in a woman's cheeks. The darting interplay of conscience and desire, first indicated through six external movements, is then "translated" into six verbal statements, the pairs bracketed with hilarious appropriateness ("look'd towards the door" — "*What would the world say?*"; "turn'd pale" — "*I should drop down, if I look'd at it*"; "recovered her natural colour" — "*There can be no sin in looking at it*"; "blushed worse than ever" — "*I will look at it*"). The teasing game of correspondences between inner and outer, mental and material, that we have already noted in *Tristram Shandy* is delightfully evident here. Long before Faulkner, Sterne adopts italics for a new convention of designating interior speech, but his very characterization of the six lines as a "translation" of gestural language suggests that the verbal formulation, however meticulous, is not quite the thing itself. We come closer here to the subtle movements of consciousness than the novel will bring us until Joyce and Proust, yet the strategy of presentation also reminds us that mercurial consciousness, which can express itself involuntarily in the contraction and dilation of the fine capillaries in the skin, is not necessarily or entirely verbal.

No critic has grapsed the paradoxicality of Sterne's self-mocking realism so firmly as Jean-Jacques Mayoux. "If every representation," Mayoux writes, "is in some degree parody, is not every parody in danger of becoming in some degree representative?" This ingenious formula suggests why the enterprise of mimesis is intrinsically comic, playful, and — in the philosophic sense — absurd for Sterne, and why, therefore, there is an ultimate difference in kind between his ostentatiously coy rendering of gesture and thought and the modern attempt to provide a "transcription" of consciousness in the various techniques of interior monologue. The effect of Sterne's method is of course enormously amusing but also disorienting, for while the purported realism of previous literature is repeatedly exposed as absurd, what is patently absurd at times strangely conforms to the lineaments of reality. Mayoux continues: "We never quite touch absolute reality. We come close to it only by signs more or less inadequate, of which the most immediate, the most powerful, correspond to our intuitions, and the most hackneyed are frozen in the code we call culture. Culture masks what would perhaps be reality; and the nostalgia for reality is one of the liveliest of Sterne's sentiments."

This is beautifully observed, though the notion of intuition needs to be extended beyond its usual sense. It is true that *Tristram Shandy* repeatedly creates channels for the flow of intuition, ranging from the imagination of fleshly desire to the impulse of creaturely sympathy. Perhaps the simplest illustration is Trim's kitchen lecture on mortality (5, 7), where a stark gesture, the dropping of a hat, puts the corporal's listeners in touch for a fleeting moment, immediately qualified by irony, with the actual meaning of Bobby's death. Gesture makes a connection with feelings masked or deflected by culture, but even the intuition triggered by gesture is not immediate, for a gesture is itself a mediation, caught up only a little less than spoken language in the fine mesh of culture. (Hats, after all, are made by hatters and worn in certain culturally determined circumstances; falling as an image of death is an agreed-upon sign; and the casting down of the top-piece in any case merely punctuates the rhythmic rhetoric of Trim's speech.) I think Mayoux is right in claiming that Sterne associates intuition with our closest approximations of reality, but since Sterne equally recognizes that all experience is mediated by mental processes, themselves conditioned by culture, he also frequently evokes the restless dynamic of the mind interacting with itself as the indisputable reality we inhabit, and thus his extreme consciousness of artifice and reader response becomes an instrument of realism. Here culture is a "mask" because it numbs the mind's awareness of its own liveliness, cripples the creativity of the imagination by accustoming it to work perfunctorily with fixed stereotypes.

The ultimate approximation of reality in *Tristram Shandy*, I would argue, is in the zany and unpredictable engendering of associations that springs the mind loose from its conventional set, enables it to experience its own athletic vitality. Sterne's method reminds us that the irrepressible world of fantasy is, at least from one point of view, our most humanly familiar reality. Many moments in *Tristram Shandy* are neither narration nor commentary nor expository digression but odd invitations for the mind to move in the most unexpected ways, the materials of fantasy being delicately coaxed into the light of consciousness.

Thus, the fifth chapter of volume 8 begins with a brief, enigmatic reflection on why women are attracted to weavers, gardeners, and gladiators (because they work with beams, sticks, and swords?), or to a man with a shriveled leg (the impotence theme once more). Sterne then proceeds, by the obscurest of connections, to a disquisition on water drinkers:

> A water-drinker, provided he is a profess'd one, and does it without
> fraud or covin, is precisely in the same predicament: not that,
> at first sight, there is any consequence, or shew of logic in it,
> "That a rill of water dribbling through my inward parts, should
> light up a torch in my *Jenny's*——"

— The proposition does not strike one; on the contrary, it seems to run opposite to the natural workings of causes and effects —

But it shews the weakness and imbecility of human reason.

— "And in perfect good health with it?"

— The most perfect — Madam, that friendship herself could wish me —

— "And drink nothing! — nothing but water?"

— Impetuous fluid! the moment thou pressest against the flood-gates of the brain — see how they give way! —

In swims CURIOSITY, beckoning to her damsels to follow — they dive into the centre of the current —

FANCY sits musing upon the bank, and with her eyes following the stream, turns straws and bulrushes into masts and bowsprits — And DESIRE, with vest held up to the knee in one hand, snatches at them, as they swim by her, with the other —

O ye water-drinkers! is it then by this delusive fountain, that ye have so often governed and turn'd this world about like a mill-wheel — grinding the faces of the impotent — bepowdering their ribs — be-peppering their noses, and changing sometimes even the very frame and face of nature —

The initial assertion about water drinkers, like the statement about weavers, gardeners, and gladiators that precedes it, is momentarily reminiscent in tone of the so-called essayistic passages in Fielding. With Fielding, however, logic and consequence are the constant underpinning both of the narrator's discourses and of the larger structure of the novel. Here, by contrast, we are immediately put on notice that what seems to follow logically as cause and effect may have very little to do with what actually goes on in the world of physical existence — thus a cold rill of water works aphrodisiacally in Tristram to light up a torch in his Jenny's — . Reason (what Locke calls "judgment") is imbecile when it assumes that its neat structures correspond to a reality infinitely inventive in its perverse variety. The faculty that does answer to the erratic and paradoxical nature of reality is not reason but imagination, as Sterne's method brilliantly illustrates here by breaking down the Fieldingesque disquisition into a fantasia of consciousness, graphically forcing "the flood-gates of the brain" to give way.

Starting with water drinkers (while we still puzzle over the weavers, and others before them), Sterne takes us through a series of quick shifts in focus and method of presentation that is analogous in effect to a rapid series of cinematic dissolves. What we experience before all else in the passage is the kinetic energy of the imagination itself, an energy confined and thwarted by conventional literary modes and logical methods of thought. From the instance of the consequences of water-drinking and the reflection on their illogicality, we are tumbled pell-mell into a dialogue between Tristram and Madam. Sterne's ubiquitous "eavesdropped effect" is acutely felt here. On a second reading we can begin to make out what Tristram and Madam are really saying to each other, but the fragmentariness of communication persists, the teasing sense that, as in ordinary life, we simply cannot get full enough information to draw conclusions with the certainty we would like. Tristram has hardly got his dialogue with Madam under way before he shifts — for a moment, as in a film dissolve, we do not realize it is a shift — into a formal apostrophe to water.

The apostrophe, in turn, with the metaphor of floodgates acting as a trigger, immediately flips into a weird allegorical landscape in which capitalized female figures of FANCY and DESIRE sit on a riverbank while CURIOSITY and her entourage of water-nymphs go diving into the stream. All this began, one recalls, with an interior rivulet coursing toward Tristram's virile member, and so the bucolic scene appropriately is a sexual fantasy in which FANCY — a term used by Sterne in approximate synonymity with fantasy, wit, and imagination — follows the illogical metamorphosis of sexual physiology itself by turning fragile straws and bulrushes into phallically swollen masts and bowsprits. DESIRE, in a suitable state of undress, shows herself a true sister to Bridget and the fair Beguine by snatching at these passing beams born of motes.

Just as the allegory is approaching the climactic essence of all true love-romances, the narrator breaks off with a dash, as in the amours of Bridget and the Beguine, and again he leaps to new ground — an apostrophe to water drinkers. This final apostrophe sweeps through a field of reference so wide and wild that the effect is of a comic phantasmagoria. The stream that has already been turned into an image of male potency here becomes a global and historical source of power, of aggressive energy, turning the world around like a mill wheel, "changing sometimes even the very frame and face of nature" (Sterne's "Freudian" intuition could hardly be better illustrated). Equally noteworthy is the way this last paragraph literally defies ordinary logic — already explicitly abused — by suddenly crashing the fantasy of virility that has informed the whole passage against the author's recurrent preoccupation with impotence, the impotent emerging from the collision here with faces ground and noses be-peppered, like poor Tristram himself.

The narrator's erratic progress is amusing, titillating, and by this point we no longer know quite what to make of it, perhaps are no longer intend-ed to know. The zigzag movement of the passage, one might observe, is unsteadily but perceptibly outward toward an expanding horizon of imagination — from a trickle of water in inward parts to a generalization and expostulation, to a stream bearing straws turned to bowsprits, to the great world spun around like a millwheel. One of the general aims of Sterne's method, I would suggest, is to make us repeatedly aware of the infinite horizon of the imagination. Since infinity can hardly be contained in a finite nar-rative form, what Sterne must do is constantly cut back sharply from the expansive associative movement of his prose through the sudden disjuncture of a dash — and return us to the small world of his comic actors. Here, we cut from the "frame and face of nature" to a very brief exchange between Yorick and Eugenius, and then, as a fitting conclusion to the chapter, Tristram's resolution "never to read any book but my own, as long as I live." The horizon evoked, however, does not entirely fade: its constant presence in the novel is one major reason why this elaborately rendered world of trivialities and frustrations nevertheless imparts to the reader a peculiar sense of comic liberation. Shandean man is everywhere in the fetters of circumstance but everywhere the imagination is free; the blind forceps of reality may crush one's nose, or whatever, to a pulp, but the mind can still spin Slawkenbergian fantasies of a man with a proboscis so enormous that it mesmerizes an entire city.

What I should like to stress about this whole bizarre procedure of Sterne's, here and elsewhere, is how far it takes us from anything like novelistic nar-ration without ever really abandoning the enterprise of the novelist. Sterne is in fact fascinated by the challenge of rendering nuanced interaction of charac-ters in intimate social settings, of conveying the complex feel of quotidian experience, and his own response to that challenge of mimesis is in several ways more subtle and convincing than any previous representation of reality in a novel. He is keenly aware, however, that mimesis is a task of Sisyphus, and he surrounds the "reality" of the little Shandy world with the constant swirl and eddy of another reality — his mind's and ours. This latter reality, he knows, is in some of its essential aspects either preverbal or metalinguistic, but he is able to implicate us in its internal dynamism through the ingenious ways by which he manipulates language and the typographical appurtenances of the printed word. *Tristram Shandy* is as much an act of pure play as any novel ever written, but as with other kinds of games, it is play that makes us strenuously rehearse some of the vital processes by which we must live in reality. In this early but ultimate instance of self-reflexive fiction, the many mirrors of the novel set to catch its own operations also give us back the image of the mind in action; and at a moment when dominant intellectual assumptions had seemed to subvert philosophically the realistic aspiration of literature, literary self-consciousness paradoxically proves to be a technique of realism as well.

Sterne and Swift:
Augustan Continuities

Max Byrd

It is possible to speak of the advantages of influence as well as the anxiety. In recent theoretical speculations, elaborating what might be called the poetics of neurosis, Harold Bloom has proposed a view of literary history as a series of baroque, subliminal psychic rivalries between modern poets and their predecessors. "Belated" modern poets, he contends, are at once inhibited and inspired by the accomplishments of earlier writers; they fall back from the challenge of an overpowering tradition and can free themselves to write only by taking arms against a sea of fathers. They take arms and by "misreading" end them. To find his own voice, that is, the filial poet must distort or reinterpret the "precursor" who tyrannizes his imagination, much as Blake recasts *Paradise Lost* to make Satan the hero and Milton the poet of the devil's party. What Bloom calls "anxiety" W. Jackson Bate more accurately and dramatically terms "the burden of the past," using as example the specific historical situation of mid- and later eighteenth-century England, when "originality" and "novelty" for the first time become conscious critical ideals and young writers feel an urgent pressure to differ from earlier writers, by sheer force of singularity if nothing else.

Laurence Sterne's extravagant assault upon literary convention has sometimes caused him to be placed among these anxious experimental writers—among pre-Romantics like Ossian, Chatterton, and Blake—but Sterne's originality, for all its subversion of convention, has finally more to do with eccentricity than experiment. He belongs in the main to an earlier generation of writers; his point of view and, so far as we can judge them,

From *Johnson and His Age* (Harvard English Studies 12), edited by James Engell. © 1984 by the President and Fellows of Harvard College. Harvard University Press, 1984.

his intentions are profoundly conservative, hard to distinguish from those of Johnson, Pope, or Swift. In spite of the celebrated "oddness," Sterne seems less like someone striking out a new path than like someone cartwheeling back and forth across familiar terrain, merely capering to absurd extremes. Indeed, in his self-absorption, in his effort to use the novel to establish or clarify his own identity, Sterne scarcely looks up to see what is being written around him; his letters and books are striking for their lack of reference to contemporary literature, and he seems unaware even of the existence of his immediate predecessors, Fielding and Richardson. His glance instead turns automatically to the past, to the writers of what D. W. Jefferson has called "the tradition of learned wit"; and his use of these writers—his cockeyed imitation of their best voices and gags—conveys nothing at all of anxiety, everything of irreverent glee.

Of all the writers of that tradition, Swift appears to have exerted the most extensive influence upon Sterne. In what follows, however, I attempt not to trace the categories of that influence in detail, only to suggest how thematic continuities tie Sterne, loosely but by a line of wit, to Swift and to certain Augustan preoccupations.

The fundamental difference between Sterne and Swift may be felt in their characteristic images for the brain—that extensive, pleasant ocean in the Sternean scheme which can accommodate a flotilla of thoughts like Dr. Slop's "without sail or ballast . . . millions of which, as your worship knows, are every day swimming quietly in the middle of the thin juice of a man's understanding, without being carried backwards or forwards, till some little gusts of passion or interest drive them to one side." Sterne, indeed, makes a leitmotiv of such images: no writer has ever described the inside of our heads so literally. In *Tristram Shandy* the "spare places of our brains" are capacious beyond all imagination (3, 20). They can contain a city square of nerves, converging on the cerebellum like streets and alleys (2, 19); Toby's head can be like the inside of a Savoyard's box or filled with wet tinder or, more wonderfully still, "like a smoak-jack;—the funnel unswept, and the ideas whirling round and round about in it, all obfuscated and darkened over with fuliginous matter" (3, 19). "Such a head!" Tristram exclaims, identifying the real setting of the novel: "—would to heaven! my enemies only saw the inside of it" (3, 38).

By contrast, Swift does not simply arrive at this inner space in the flicker of a simile. His entry is accomplished by the officious Reason, "with Tools for cutting, and opening, and mangling, and piercing." And when the brain is finally laid open and dissected, he draws our attention not to its spaciousness but to its disappointing "Defects . . . in Number and Bulk." Or if we consider ideas to be like the mist that rises from a dunghill, then, contends the narrator of *A Tale of a Tub*, "it will follow, that as the Face of Nature never produces Rain, but when it is overcast and disturbed, so Human Understanding, seated in the Brain, must be troubled and overspread by Vapours, ascending from the lower Faculties, to water the Invention, and render it fruitful." Elsewhere, in the course of explaining the usefulness of quilted caps, he repeats "the Opinion of Choice *Virtuosi*, that the Brain is only a Crowd of little Animals, but with Teeth and Claws extremely sharp, and therefore, cling together in the Contexture we behold, like the Picture of *Hobbes*'s *Leviathan*, or like Bees in perpendicular swarm upon a Tree, or like a Carrion corrupted into Vermin, still preserving the Shape and Figure of the Mother Animal."

Every comparison of Swift and Sterne turns into a contrast like this, in which an initial similarity of purpose collapses, as here Sterne's vividly distinct images, his rapidfire fantasy, shrivel before Swift's relentless development of simile into monstrous analogy. Sterne himself makes comparisons with Swift into contrasts: unlike Swift, he tells one correspondent, he has not yet been persecuted by his enemies into great fame; unlike Swift, he tells another, who has warned him against indecent humor, he will be cautious—"I deny I have gone as farr as Swift—He keeps a due distance from Rabelais—& I keep a due distance from him—Swift has said a hundred things I durst Not Say—Unless I was Dean of St. Patricks." But this is not to say that Swift exerts no influence on him. To the contrary, in a general way Sterne clearly identifies with him, seeing himself as a second Anglo-Irish clergyman frustrated by the politics of the church, too clever for his own good, writing himself out of favor and into scandal as Swift did in *A Tale of a Tub*. He describes proudly to Eliza how old Lord Bathurst, the former patron of Pope and Swift, came up to him in London and declared, "Despairing ever to find their equals, it is some years since I have closed my accounts, and shut up my books, with thoughts of never opening them again: but you have kindled a desire in me of opening them once more before I die; which I now do; so go home and dine with me." The *Journal to Eliza* itself appears to have been inspired by Swift's *Journal to Stella*, which was published in 1766, the year that Sterne met Eliza.

As a writer, Sterne responded chiefly to *A Tale of a Tub* (*Gulliver's Travels* seems hardly to have interested him), and what he responded to is very clear: of all the major works usually cited as Sterne's sources—*Gargantua and Pantagruel, Don Quixote*, Montaigne's *Essays*—the formal elements of *Tristram Shandy* are most nearly replicated in the *Tale*. No other source so closely resembles it in details of structure and device—the digressions piled precariously upon digressions, the mock-scholastic parodies of literary decorum (Swift's endless Apology, Dedication, Preface, and Introduction), the volleys against critics, the proposals for other books, and the division of emphasis between actual narration and the encroaching personality of the narrator. Even certain recurrent images of the *Tale*—brains, horses, noses—appear again in *Tristram Shandy*. At the most general level these resemblances disappear, of course—Swift is writing a satire and Sterne a novel—but similar forms sometimes have a way of generating similar themes. Sterne's bawdry, his interest in language as a subject of interpretation and corruption, and his view of madness undoubtedly have many sources, including most importantly his own enigmatic and self-afflicting personality; but his predispositions to those themes are surely mobilized by Swift's example, even if from a common starting point they tend to go racing in utterly different directions.

"Walter is wise, he is witty, he is humane," writes John Traugott, "—and he is mad." "Is Uncle Toby mad too?" John Preston asks, comparing him to Swift's demented Jack. All of the inhabitants of Shandy Hall, observes V. S. Pritchett, "live shut up in the madhouse of their own imaginations, oysters itching voluptuously upon the pearl within." "The real point about Walter and Toby," says Michael DePorte, "is not so much that Sterne thinks them mad, or even that most contemporary readers would have thought them mad; the point is rather that given the psychiatric criteria of the day they *are* mad."

This is not true, of course. Swift's Hack narrator in the *Tale* is a genuine madman by eighteenth-century criteria, a self-confessed "student" of Bedlam, a projector whose "imaginations are hard-mouth'd, and exceedingly disposed to run away with his *Reason*, which I have observed from long Experience, to be a very light Rider, and easily shook off." His actual madness reflects a cultural crisis of enormous proportions to Swift's mind, a destructive folly that is willful, poisonous, and sinful, and it will serve as an image of self-deception and blindness throughout Swift's career, from the Calvinist Jack and the raging Peter to the Bedlamite Yahoos of *Gulliver's Travels*. But if "madness" is a term almost unavoidable in a discussion of Swift's work, it occurs to few contemporaries of Sterne, who prefer instead to see his eccentric heroes as Rabelaisian humorists rather than as madmen. It is true that Tristram describes himself as subject to the changes of the moon and finds that he, too, will be led astray by his "pads" (hobbyhorses): "sometimes, to my shame be it spoken, I take somewhat longer journies than what a wise man would think altogether right" (1, 8). And "Shandy" is Yorkshire dialect for crack-brained, addled. But to be long on the road, to be addled, not to be wise—these confessions hardly bear comparison with the tragic madness of Swift's fools. And in any case, the literal degradation of eighteenth-century insanity—the shocking excremental squalor that so intensifies the figurative energy of Swift's satire—plays no part in Sterne's vision, which domesticates folly to mere eccentricity or humor, the harmless single-mindedness that he and his readers intend when they speak of "Cervantick satyr." By contrast, Swift's madmen are not only degraded, but destructive: drawing upon the ancient tradition of madness as a link to supernatural power, he presents the mad world as dangerous and revolutionary; his madmen in the *Tale* are murderous princes and generals like Henry IV, subversive philosophers like Hobbes, dissenting enthusiasts like the Puritans; and as any English reader with a memory of the Civil Wars would understand, they daily threaten the stability of church and state. Against this vision of public crisis, Sterne can only set the private impotence of Toby and his monomania, a sentimental saint, like Don Quixote insane in just one way and all the more virtuous in every other.

Nonetheless, if the idea of madness in Sterne's works is primarily a critical metaphor imposed from without and not a thematic motif as in Swift, it is imposed so often because it discloses a moral issue central to both writers. The association of ideas that Sterne took from Locke and made into a comic device occurs in a context of irrational behavior that verges, as many readers have felt, on madness: Locke's gallery of victims who are tyrannized by their fixed habits of association—as Tristram tells us his parents are—grows progressively more bizarre, until the principle of association becomes a kind of "unreasonableness" that is, Locke says with unusual anger, perhaps our "greatest" source of "error." Such "unnatural" and habitual associations as we all develop are at the "root" of madness, he declares, adding, "I shall be pardoned for calling it by so harsh a name as madness, when it is considered that opposition to reason deserves that name, and is really madness; and there is scarce a man so free from it, but that if he should always, on all occasions, argue or do as in some cases he constantly does, would not be thought fitter for Bedlam than civil conversation."

In Locke's hands this unreasonableness constitutes a criticism of human nature. In Sterne's hands it constitutes a criticism of reason. Or rather, of the view that makes reason sovereign over human nature. For no principle of logic, no "natural" connection, is strong enough to penetrate Walter's mesh of theory or Toby's bunkers, or to make Tristram follow an orderly pattern of narration; even that notorious eighteenth-century symbol of divine and human reason, the clock, takes its place in a wildly unnatural association of ideas. If we object that Sterne is merely describing obsession or the Renaissance psychology of "humors," his explicit references to Locke's *Essay* still complicate what would otherwise be familiar techniques of comedy, and encourage us to speak seriously, even philosophically, of Shandean eccentricity, as we cannot, for example, of Sir Epicure Mammon's greed or Lord Emsworth's dottiness about pigs. The emphasis Sterne brings to bear on language and interpretation, moreover, connects his work to the Cervantic tradition, in which madness becomes not a matter of reason or unreason but a matter of point of view. (It can be no accident that the Shakespearean play to which *Tristram Shandy* most often alludes is *Hamlet*, where themes of interpretation, illusion, and madness are paramount.) Neither Cervantes or Sterne, of course, goes so far as to say that reason has no part in our makeup; but in the mirror of Toby's monomania, in Walter's approximately plausible theories, and the Don's ready explanations of enchantment, they obviously parody its operation and its claims; and at extreme moments their parody raises the possibility that reason bears no necessary relationship to reality at all. "Herein seems to lie the difference between idiots and madmen," Locke says: "that madmen put wrong ideas together, and so make wrong propositions, but argue and reason right from them; but idiots make very few or no propositions, and reason scarce at all." The difference, that is, lies finally between Locke's thoroughly Augustan position that madness is "wrong"— the moral connotations of his language recall Swift, who holds his Bedlamites accountable for choosing to be "well-deceived"—and Sterne's more equivocal suggestion that every consciousness contains a fiction, every subjectivity a truth.

The issue, finally, may be put into the classical terms of the age. The great criticism of Swift, Johnson, and Locke is that although reason enables us to apprehend reality, imagination blinds us to it. "There is no man whose imagination does not sometimes predominate over his reason," Imlac insists in Johnson's moving portrait of a madman's delusion, "who can regulate his attention wholly by his will, and whose ideas will come and go at his command. No man will be found in whose mind airy notions do not sometimes tyrannise, and force him to hope or fear beyond the limits of sober probability." It has been argued that Sterne's view of imagination is sufficiently esemplastic to include him in the coming generation of writers, like Blake, Coleridge, and Wordsworth, who would transform the imagination into a creative principle, a moral and aesthetic standard higher than sober reason. But in his sermons, those indispensable commentaries on his fiction, Sterne speaks of imagination in a voice that we can hardly distinguish from Johnson's: "Will the coolest and most circumspect say, when pleasure has taken full possession of his heart, that no thought nor purpose shall arise there, which he would have concealed? — In those loose and unguarded moments the imagination is not always at command — in spite of reason and reflection, it will forceably carry him sometimes whither he would not." ("All power of fancy over reason," Imlac declares, "is a degree of insanity"). And in his whole comedy of hobbyhorses, which carry Tristram (like Swift's loose rider) "whither he would not," we are still very far from the prevailing value of sensibility, the belief that irrationality releases some inward power and guides us toward a higher consciousness. In his literal pictures of the brain — as in Swift's — we are even further from something like Wordsworth's vision on Mt. Snowdon of "the perfect image of a mighty mind, / Of one that feeds upon infinity," a mind that resembles the highest possibility of the poet's mind. For Sterne's vision of mind reaches no higher than hobbyhorses or the "several receptacles, cells, cellules, domiciles, dormitories, refectories, and spare places of our brains" (3, 20).

Sterne's presentations of madness lead no one toward an elevated consciousness or a profounder reality. Or to put it more positively, we might say that Sterne, like Johnson, displays the classic Augustan faith that human nature is primarily social, that reality (not hell) is other people. If his idea of community is sentimental and nonhierarchical, in contrast to the usual Augustan view, he nonetheless shares the impulse that makes Imlac advise the mad astronomer to forsake his solitude and to correct his madness by conversation and society. Thus, there is misunderstanding in every social exchange in *Tristram Shandy*, but not alienation. There is subjectivity, but not solitude. A sense of human limitations, given in an elegiac tone and defined by the familiar Augustan terms of time and death, crowds his characters together and renders them foolish and mad only in the ordinary human sense. From another point of view Sterne, like Swift, is simply drawing on a view of madness traditional among preachers: like other Augustans, he is writing a comic version of Ecclesiastes.

On two occasions, however, Sterne does describe actual madness. The account of Maria, the peasant madwoman whom Tristram meets near Moulins, belongs to a subgenre invented and perfected in "the age of sensibility": the portrait of madness designed to elicit neither scorn nor awe, but quivering, tearful pity. This is the same Maria who afterward triggers Yorick's apostrophe to "sensibility" in *A Sentimenal Journey* and whose sisters the Man of Feeling visits in dreamlike Bedlam cells: a stock figure of bathos, adumbrated perhaps in Richardson's Clarissa, grotesquely distorted in the madwomen of Gothic fiction to come. In Maria the idea of madness as willful, blamable folly has disappeared; the manic energy, at once menacing and obscene, of Swift's madhouses has given way to passivity and melancholy. Unfettered, she roams far from the uproar of both Shandy Hall and Bedlam. Sterne does, however, connect her tenuously to the supernatural by the fact that, although no one has taught her to pipe, she has somehow learned the service to the Virgin Mary. And she combines this hint of literal inspiration with the eroticism that is never far from such feminine vulnerability: "she was beautiful; and if ever I felt the full force of an honest heart-ache, it was the moment I saw her" (9, 24). Maria appears to exist primarily in fact, to provoke the repressed sexuality of her admirers (she is herself frustrated in love). Yorick will collapse in self-ravishment, vibrating to the great "Sensorium" of feeling that her madness has revealed. More typically, Tristram will retreat to a disarming psychological distance, calling his initial heartache by that most Augustan of pejoratives, "my enthusiasm," and breaking her spell with a crude, insensible joke:

> MARIA look'd wistfuly for some time at me, and then at her goat — and then at me — and then at her goat again, and so on, alternately —
> — Well, *Maria*, said I softly — What resemblance do you find?
> (3, 24)

Madness, in short, turns to bawdry, as does everything else in Sterne's world, releasing suggestion if not meaning. In this regard, Sterne may be said to occupy a position halfway between Rabelais and the Victorians: if the subject of sex is never more than a page away in his work, yet it is never rendered steadily or directly. The element of fantasy present in everyone's sexuality appears to suffuse Sterne's: he imagines strangely bodiless flirtations, concentrated with excruciating sensitivity on extremities, tips of fingers, pulses. In such jokes as Toby's bewilderment over the "right end of a woman," we encounter Sterne's characteristic combination of bravado and impotence (2, 7), in the tremulous indecencies of *Journal to Eliza* and *A Sentimental Journey* a prolonged but superficial hysteria. Swift obviously stands far closer to Rabelais: there is nothing of the nudging elbow in his humor, nothing of Sterne's characteristic wink and snigger. But there is little of Rabelais's gaiety, either. Swift's indecent humor, when it concerns sexuality, strikes most readers as coarse rather than direct, without pleasure. And when it grows scatological, most readers pull back from the grim anger it discharges, an anger that sometimes seems directed at the sheer inescapable fact of the human body's functions. In his account of the Aeolist priests, for example, Swift's Hack first explains that large funnels stuck up their posteriors bring on the inspiration of strong winds and eloquent eructations. More impressive still, he adds, are the "*Female* Officers, whose Organs were understood to be better disposed for the Admission of those Oracular *Gusts*, as entring and passing up thro' a Receptacle of greater Capacity, and causing also a Pruriency by the Way, such as with due Management, hath been refined from a Carnal, into a Spiritual Extasie." This sardonic refinement ("refined" is surely the most common adjective in the *Tale*) has long been recognized as Swift's version of sublimation, the displacement of psychic effects from an appropriate to a disguised object, although Swift states it in Aristotelian rather than psychological terms: "the Corruption of the Senses is the Generation of the Spirit." Nor does he limit its application to female pruriency. As the Hack narrator of the *Tale* undertakes to survey the uses of madness in a commonwealth, he begins with the case of a "certain Great Prince" (Henry IV of France), who suddenly raises a mighty army and fleet and threatens universal conquest. "It was afterwards discovered, that the Movement of this whole Machine had been directed by an absent *Female*, whose Eyes had raised a Protuberancy, and before Emission, she was removed into an Enemy's Country . . . The very same Principle that influences a *Bully* to break the Windows of a Whore, who has jilted him, naturally stirs up a Great Prince to raise mighty Armies, and dream nothing but Sieges, Battles, and Victories."

Whatever the remoter origins of Uncle Toby—the sentimental memory of Sterne's soldier-father or the eccentric Captain Robert Hinde proposed by some scholars—it is impossible to avoid seeing Swift's version of sublimation at work in him, spurring the hobbyhorse of siegecraft, his "Fancy . . . *astride* on his Reason" as firmly as any Bedlam inmate's. ("Most Kinds of Diversion in Men, Children, and other Animals," Swift sardonically observes, "are an Imitation of Fighting.") Sterne makes the connection between repressed sexuality and warfare almost as plain, in fact, as Swift does: when Trim utters the words "A Rood and a half of ground to do what they would with," Toby blushes immoderately, and a moment later Tristram draws the necessary comparison, adding only a teasing note on the importance of privacy to miniature warfare: "Never did lover post down to a belov'd mistress with more heat and expectation, than my uncle *Toby* did, to enjoy this selfsame thing in private . . . The idea of not being seen, did not a little contribute to the idea of pleasure preconceived in my uncle *Toby*'s mind" (2, 5).

For Sterne this displacement of erotic energy apparently represents no more than a joke on human nature, a Shandean variation on a topos that, one way or another, stretches back to the *Iliad*. For Swift, however, the joke is made through clenched teeth. Its serious point is that our politics derive from our illogical psychology, that our collective corruption has its source in the ease with which our lower faculties control our higher. More seriously still, such sublimation reveals a moral error: the preference of illusion to truth; for we know these things about ourselves, or ought to, and yet choose to remain mired in appetite, willfully blind to realities. Swift makes the consequences of this self-deceit as violent and repellent as he can; he pitches it all in the place of excrement, and with the climactic image of Bedlam hospital and its iron bars he makes clear that when we choose this way we choose to be enslaved, not to be free. But Sterne simply turns away from the satiric possibilities implicit in the preference of illusion over truth. His voice returns no echo of Swift's fierceness. Toby's mock warfare leaves flies unharmed and widows unravished. Apart from that rood and a half of sublimation, in fact, Sterne's bawdry far more than Swift's depends upon ambiguity and ambivalence, matters for linguistic rather than moral interpretation.

At the practical, larcenous level from which novelists usually regard other fiction, Sterne unquestionably discovered in Swift's allegory of the brothers Martin, Peter, and Jack the problem of interpretation in its most suggestive form. For their father's will had, of course, expressly commanded the three brothers never to alter the appearance of their inherited coats; but motivated by lust — by their desire to court three grand ladies — they concoct a series of sophistic rereadings of the will that begins with shoulder knots and oral tradition, proceeds to gold lace and Aristotle's *de Interpretatione* ("which has the Faculty of teaching its Readers to find out a Meaning in every Thing but it self"), and concludes with satin linings and sheer forgery. And though Swift's satiric target here is primarily the Roman Catholic church, he makes the same general point throughout his career: words have at once a single meaning and endless meanings. Like Locke, he holds to the view that words should mean definite things, precisely and obviously. ("There are some poets, Kipling for example," writes W. H. Auden, "whose relation to language reminds one of a drill sergeant: the words are taught to wash behind their ears, stand properly at attention and execute complicated maneuvers, but at the cost of never being allowed to think for themselves.") But unlike Locke, who finds the problem in the inherent ambiguity of language itself, Swift blames instead its corrupt users — the politicians, priests, and rabble who pervert what can and should be clear. "*I charge and command my said three sons,*" booms the will, "*to wear no sort of* Silver Fringe *upon or about their said Coats* . . . However, after some Pause the Brother so often mentioned for his Erudition, who was well Skill'd in Criticisms, had found in a certain Author, which he said should be nameless, that the same Word which in the Will is called *Fringe*, does also signifie a *Broom-stick*."

Sterne, no one has ever doubted, delights in the ambiguity that so discourages Swift. In Sterne's world, words never stand still for a single meaning: they dart continually like seabirds into our subconscious, returning every moment with fresh and outrageous evidence of our disposition to pervert. And while Swift directs his satire at the brothers' willingness to make words mean whatever they want—in the service of power, vanity, and illusion as well as lust—Sterne limits the alternative meanings to a single kind: whatever we say, we are thinking of sex.

> ——Here are two senses, cried *Eugenius*, as we walk'd along, point-
> ing with the fore finger of his right hand to the word *Crevice*,
> in the fifty-second page of the second volume of this book of
> books, —— here are two senses, —— quoth he. —— And here are two
> roads, replied I, turning short upon him, —— a dirty and a clean
> one, —— which shall we take? —— The clean, —— by all means,
> replied *Eugenius*. *Eugenius*, said I, stepping before him, and laying
> my hand upon his breast, —— to define —— is to distrust. (3, 31)

Crevices, whiskers, noses: fanned by the south winds of the libido, every word turns gently over to reveal another meaning. So infectious, in fact, is Tristram's habit of sexualizing his language that after a time no word at all seems innocent. Scholars read with dictionaries of slang open beside them ("toby" means "penis"), hobbyhorses turn stud, and a sentence justifying digressions can bring explication to a blushing halt: "when a man is telling his story in the strange way I do mine, he is obliged continually to be going backwards and forwards to keep all tight together in the reader's fancy" (6, 33). Tristram says, quite truthfully, that he depends "upon the cleanliness of my readers' imaginations" (3, 31).

Swift indulges in no such trust. If Sterne offers us a choice of meanings, either possible, for his part Swift insists that interpretation aims at nothing less than truth. Peter, having locked away the will and seized power over his brothers, thrusts a piece of bread before them and, in a parody of tran-substantiation, calls it mutton. They protest that the mutton strangely resembles a twelve-penny loaf. "*Look ye, Gentlemen*, cries Peter in a Rage, *to convince you, what couple of blind, positive, ignorant, wilful Puppies you are, I will use but this plain Argument; by G*——*, it is true, good, natural Mutton as any in* Leaden-Hall Market; *and G*—— *confound you both eternally, if you offer to believe otherwise*. Such a thundring Proof as this, left no farther Room for Objection: The two Unbelievers began to gather and pocket up their Mistake, as hastily as they could." This is quixotic madness gone sour; fic-tion turned to lies. Worse still, it is a moral failing for which language is not responsible. Here, of course, Swift assigns responsibility for misrepresenting truth to his characters, the mad Peter and his cowardly brothers, and by ex-tension to the religious factions they represent. But as so often happens in his work, the page never contains his anger. Elsewhere and generally throughout the *Tale*, responsibility for misinterpretation widens to include not only the Hack and his puppets, but also the "Gentle Reader" and flawed human nature, torn perpetually between the state of being a knave or a well-deceived fool. "I am wonderfully well acquainted with the present Relish of Courteous Readers," says the Hack in an ostensible compliment to us; "and have often observed with singular Pleasure, that a *Fly* driven from a *Honey-pot*, will immediately, with very good Appetite alight, and finish his Meal on an Excrement."

Sterne may have taken from Swift the technique of reaching out thus to include the reader in the "conversation" of the book, but he never duplicates the suffocating intimacy Swift so ferociously achieves: his clowning references to "Madam" and "Sir" and "Your Reverences" create only a curiously impersonal familiarity. Nor does he duplicate the technique of irony that places so crushing a burden of interpretation on the reader. For Swift's irony finally extends the question of interpretation beyond the action or the texts within his texts: it challenges the reader directly to understand the writer himself, as a person, as a character, and it works to ensure that he cannot. The relationship between author and reader is the ultimate question of truthful interpretation that Swift raises, and raises only to deny. Beneath Tristram's mad dashes, the chatter and puppyish cajoling, we detect a self in the making, a self engaged, as Sterne declared to David Garrick, in an act of self-portrait, a personality that we (and Sterne) can eventually "read." A far stronger self lies beneath Swift's metamorphoses—a face glimpsed and lost at every moment—but it is the last illusion to think that we can know him.

The issue of truth in interpretation, however, may be seen in another way, through the memorable vividness of a stylistic interest shared by both writers. Readers have long noticed that Swift's brilliant use of metaphor is not without a characteristic tension between literal and figurative meanings. There is, for example, the absurdity of Peter's claim that bread is mutton, which mocks one metaphor with another and plays them both against our literal experience of bread and meat. There is, as well, the absurdity of effect when dunces take a figurative expression and act upon it literally, so that Jack, having described a skin of parchment (the Bible) as "Cloth," wraps it about his head "for a Night-cap when he went to Bed, and for an Umbrello in rainy Weather." Or when the sages of Laputa carry about great packs of implements and things to display in place of speech. Or when the tailors of the *Tale* mistake a metaphor for reality and thus hold "the Universe to be a large *Suit of Cloaths*." Swift's practice, moreover, is to allow his misreaders to carry their literalizations as far as possible, to construct systems from them, and to fashion a metaphorical reality that at best misleads, at worst blasphemes. Hence the Aeolists, taking etymology literally, misunderstand completely the spiritual expression "inspiration" and transform it into the belchings and eructations of Dissent. Hence too the metaphorical "devouring" of Ireland that so offends the Modest Proposer leads him to advocate a literal cannibalism. In all of these collisions between metaphor and truth, we are encountering Swift's wonderful, surreal inventiveness, but we are also encountering an obvious moral challenge to sift through metaphor to correctness.

Few readers can have gone far in *Tristram Shandy* without recognizing that Sterne writes as one of the incontestable masters of the comic image. I have in mind not only those precise visual images he continually creates ("a number of tall, opake words, one before another, in a right line" [3, 20]), but also the explicit comparisons that pop suddenly around the corner of the most ordinary syntax:

> others on the contrary, tuck'd up to their very chins with whips across their mouths, scouring and scampering it away like so many little party-coloured devils astride a mortgage. (1, 8)

> Humph! — said my uncle *Toby*; — tho' not accented as a note of acquiescence, — but as an interjection of that particular species of surprize, when a man, in looking into a drawer, finds more of a thing than he expected. (2, 17)

> He pick'd up an opinion, Sir, as a man in a state of nature picks up an apple. (3, 34)

There is a wealth of pleasure in such silliness. We can respond to the cleverness of the allusions to Hobbes's state of nature and to Swift's runaway horse "astride" a mortgage; we like the irrepressible bawdry by which "drawer" metamorphoses into an undergarment; or we take simple pleasure in the childlike literalness with which Sterne revitalizes abstractions like mortgages and opinions. But absent completely is that Swiftian tension between literal (that is, true) and figurative meanings, between moral correctness and self-deception. Absent, too, is Swift's habit of developing a metaphor into a system. Sterne's images come in a random, unpredictable fashion and disappear like bubbles. Even where Sterne does exploit the tension between literal and figurative, it is not for any moral purpose: Toby misunderstands every possible expression that touches upon siegecraft — "As *Yorick* pronounced the word *point blank*, my uncle *Toby* rose up to say something upon projectiles" (4,

26). He is the true Lockean man, who takes all words in one sense only, literally or figuratively according to the inappropriateness of the context ("You shall lay your finger upon the place — said my uncle *Toby*. — I will not touch it, however, quoth Mrs. *Wadman* to herself [9, 20]). But he is also and undeniably the good man, the very opposite of a dunce or hack, the man of sentiment whose instinctive compassion transcends all verbal language. And though his constant misinterpretations are as complete and systematic as any in the *Tale*, he follows them virtually alone, with the single disciple Trim, not as part of a mob (to use the word Swift so disliked). And in any case, there is always someone present to correct his misinterpretation and to readjust the context.

When Tristram develops a metaphor on his own, moreover, his interest in the literal is limited to the creation of those numerous personifications that are such a feature of his style; and he proceeds ordinarily not by a rigorous and obvious logic, but by a skittering process of free association. Thus he begins a chapter with a reference to Momus's famous complaint that Hephaestus's model of a man lacks a window in his breast, where his desires and secrets can be seen; he goes on to imagine Momus's window installed in real people, then in the inhabitants of the planet Mercury, who must be turned entirely to glass by the heat of the sun. But at the end Tristram himself interposes to correct the metaphor and to insure that we do not take it literally: "But this, as I said above, is not the case of the inhabitants of this earth; — our minds shine not through the body, but are wrapt up here in a dark covering of uncrystalized flesh and blood; so that if we would come to the specifick characters of them, we must go some other way to work" (1, 23). A faint preacherly tone of voice can be heard here, of course. But in general Sterne's comic images rarely raise questions of interpretation and deception as Swift's do. Rather than moral urgency, they communicate something like that delight in nonsense which is never quite unalloyed in Swift. They communicate a simple, playful joy in the manipulation of unreal words — or in W. K. Wimsatt's phrase, in the cheerful manipulation of a "heightened unreality" characteristic of the Augustan wits. Wimsatt adds, "The peculiar feat of the Augustan poet was the art of teasing unreality with the redeeming force of wit — of casting upon a welter of unreal materials a light of order and a perspective vision." To the extent that this is a moral enterprise — redeeming, ordering — Sterne's kinship may be in some doubt, despite his frequent protests that he had written nothing but moral works. To the extent, however, that Sterne, like Pope in his freest moments, simply cuts loose from literal meaning and delights in that chaotic unreality, the kinship is secure.

Nonsense precipitate, like running Lead,
That slip'd thro' Cracks and Zig-zags of the Head.

(*Dunciad*, 1.123-24)

As when a dab-chick waddles thro' the copse
On feet and wings, and flies, and wades, and hops;
So lab'ring on, with shoulders, hands, and head,
Wide as a wind-mill all his figures spread.

(*Dunciad*, 2.63-66)

——my father could never subscribe to it by any means; the very
idea of so noble, so refined, so immaterial, and so exalted a being
as the *Anima*, or even the *Animus*, taking up her residence, and
sitting dabbling, like a tad-pole, all day long, both summer, and
winter, in a puddle. (*Tristram Shandy*, 2, 19)

But it is the measure of Swift's seriousness—and sometimes of his grimness—
that he so infrequently turns his back on the literal and verisimilar, that reality
so implacably encroaches on his fantasies. If he could have known it, Sterne's
uncritical pleasure in the irrational would only have seemed to him without
moral weight and tension. Or as C. J. Rawson observes in a genuinely Shandean speculation about literary influence, "what the *Tale of the Tub* is really
parodying is Sterne, in advance."

Chronology

1713	Born in Clonmel, Ireland, to Roger and Agnes Sterne. Father an infantry officer of the lowest rank, but grandson of an archbishop of York; mother is thought to have been the daughter of a sutler. The family moves with the regiment, in England and Ireland.
1723	Sent to school in Yorkshire, where he is looked after by his uncle Richard Sterne.
1731	Father dies in Jamaica.
1733–37	Studies at Jesus College, Cambridge, on an allowance from a cousin and on a scholarship founded by his great-grandfather Sterne, at one time master of the college. B.A. in 1737 and the corollary M.A. in 1740. Reads Locke. Has severe hemorrhage of the lungs, the beginning of his incurable tuberculosis.
1737	Becomes curate of St. Ives upon graduation.
1738	Ordained priest, appointed vicar to Sutton-on-the-Forest, near York.
1740	Becomes a prebendary (canon) of York. Helped by his uncle, Dr. Jacques Sterne, precentor of York and archdeacon of Cleveland.
1740–62	Preaches at York Minster until tuberculosis causes loss of voice. Sermons very popular.
1741	Marries Elizabeth Lumley. Farms to supplement income.
1741–42	Writes political articles supporting Sir Robert Walpole for Jacques Sterne's newspaper. Presented the prebendary for North Newbald as reward. Withdraws from political writing, disgusted, making an enemy of his uncle.
1743	Publishes "The Unknown World, Verses occasioned by hearing a Pass-Bell" in *The Gentleman's Magazine*.
1747	Daughter, Lydia, born.

1747–51	Sterne relatives plague him. Dr. Jacques Sterne has Sterne's mother lodged in a prison to embarrass the son.
1759	Publishes *A Political Romance* (later renamed *The History of a Good Warm Watch-Coat*), a satire on church politics. Churchmen have the book burned. Sterne's prospects in the church dim. Mother and uncle die; wife has nervous breakdown.
1760	Publishes volumes 1 and 2 of *Tristram Shandy* at York: London edition in January. Visits London. Lionized. Presented with the parish of Griswold. Publishes *The Sermons of Mr. Yorick*, volumes 1 and 2.
1761	Volumes 3 and 4, then 5 and 6 of *Tristram Shandy* published. Moves to "Shandy Hall" at Coxwold.
1762	Tuberculosis worsens. Travels to France for drier air. In February, rumor spreads that he is dead; he is eulogized. Spends January to June in Paris, meets Diderot and other French intellectuals. In July, joined by Elizabeth Sterne and Lydia, who settle in France.
1764	Returns to York. Finishes volumes 7 and 8.
1765	Publishes volumes 7 and 8 of *Tristram Shandy*.
1765–66	Travels in France and Italy.
1766	Publishes volumes 3 and 4 of *The Sermons of Mr. Yorick* (volumes 5, 6, and 7 published posthumously by Lydia).
1767	Publishes volume 9 of *Tristram Shandy*.
	Meets Eliza Draper, wife of an East India Company official, with whom he openly carries on a flirtation until her husband calls her back to Bombay. Begins the *Journal to Eliza* (first published in 1904).
	Elizabeth and Lydia Sterne visit him at Coxwold.
	Finishes and publishes *A Sentimental Journey*. Collapses.
1768	Dies in his Bond Street lodgings in London.

Contributors

HAROLD BLOOM, Sterling Professor of the Humanities at Yale University, is the author of *The Anxiety of Influence, Poetry and Repression,* and many other volumes of literary criticism. His forthcoming study, *Freud: Transference and Authority,* attempts a full-scale reading of all of Freud's major writings. A MacArthur Prize Fellow, he is general editor of five series of literary criticism published by Chelsea House. During 1987–88, he was appointed Charles Eliot Norton Professor of Poetry at Harvard University.

DOROTHY VAN GHENT is the author of *The English Novel: Form and Function, Keats: The Myth of the Hero,* and *Willa Cather*; she is the coauthor of *The Essential Prose.*

MARTIN PRICE is Sterling Professor of English Literature at Yale University. His books include *Swift's Rhetorical Art: A Study in Structure and Meaning, To the Palace of Wisdom: Studies in Order and Energy from Dryden to Blake, Forms of Life: Character and Moral Imagination in the Novel.*

RONALD PAULSON, Professor of English at The Johns Hopkins University, has written *The Fictions of Satire, Satire and the Novel in Eighteenth-Century England, Theme and Structure in Swift's "Tale of a Tub," The Art of Hogarth, Emblem and Expression: Meaning in English Art of the Eighteenth Century,* and *Literary Landscape: Turner and Constable.*

IAN WATT, Professor of English at Stanford University, has taught both in England and in the United States, specializing in eighteenth-century literature and Joseph Conrad. His books include *The Rise of the Novel: Studies in Defoe, Richardson, and Fielding, Conrad in the Nineteenth Century,* and the forthcoming *Gothic and Comic: Two Variations on the Realistic Tradition.*

MARTIN BATTESTIN is William R. Kenan, Jr., Professor of English at the University of Virginia. He has edited the Clarendon and Wesleyan University Press editions of the works of Henry Fielding, on whom his research in eighteenth-century literature and the arts concentrates. He is the author of *The Moral Basis of Fielding's Art: A Study of Joseph Andrews* and *The Providence of Wit: Aspects of Form in Augustan Literature and the Arts.*

ROBERT ALTER, Professor of Hebrew and Comparative Literature at the University of California at Berkeley, is the author of *Rogue's Progress: Studies in the Picaresque Novel, Fielding and the Nature of the Novel, After Tradition, Partial Magic: The Novel as a Self-Conscious Genre, Defenses of the Imagination, A Lion for Love,* and *The Art of Biblical Narrative.*

MAX BYRD's work on the eighteen century includes a book on *Tristram Shandy,* a collection of essays on Defoe, as well as *Visits to Bedlam: Madness and Literature in the Eighteenth Century* and *London Transformed: Images of the City in the Eighteenth Century.* He also writes fiction.

Bibliography

Alter, Robert. "*Tristram Shandy* and the Game of Love." *The American Scholar* 37 (1968): 316–22.

Anderson, Howard. "Associationism and Wit in *Tristram Shandy*." *Philological Quarterly* 48 (1969): 27–41.

——. "*Tristram Shandy* and the Reader's Imagination." *PMLA* 86 (1971): 966–73.

——. "A Version of Pastoral: Class and Society in *Tristram Shandy*." *Studies in English Literature 1500–1900* 7 (1967): 509–29.

Baird, Theodore. "The Time-Scheme of *Tristram Shandy* and a Source." *PMLA* 51 (1936): 803–20.

Bakhtin, M. M. *The Dialogic Imagination.* Austin: University of Texas Press, 1981.

Banerjee, Chinmoy. "*Tristram Shandy* and the Association of Ideas." *Texas Studies in Literature and Language* 15 (1974): 693–706.

Battestin, Martin C. *The Providence of Wit: Aspects of Form in Augustan Literature and the Arts.* Oxford: Clarendon, 1974.

Booth, Wayne C. *The Rhetoric of Fiction.* Chicago: The University of Chicago Press, 1961.

Brissenden, R. F. *Virtue in Distress: Studies in the Novel of Sentiment from Richardson to Sade.* London: Macmillan, 1974.

Byrd, Max. *Tristram Shandy.* London: Allen & Unwin, 1985.

Cash, Arthur H. *Laurence Sterne: The Early and Middle Years.* New York: Methuen, 1975.

——. *Laurence Sterne: The Later Years.* New York: Methuen, 1987.

Cash, Arthur H. and John M. Stedmont, eds. *The Winged Skull: Papers from the Laurence Sterne Bicentenary Conference.* Kent, Ohio: Kent State University Press, 1971.

Clifford, James L., ed. *Eighteenth-Century English Literature: Modern Essays in Criticism.* New York: Oxford University Press, 1959.

Cruttwell, Patrick. "Makers and Persons." *The Hudson Review* 12 (1959–60): 487–507.

Davies, Richard A. "Tristram Shandy's Eccentric Public Orator." *English Studies in Canada* 5 (1979): 154–66.

Dobrée, Bonamy, ed. *From Anne to Victoria: Essays by Various Hands.* London: Cassell, 1937.

Donaldson, Ian. "The Clockwork Novel: Three Notes on an Eighteenth-Century Analogy." *The Review of English Studies*, 21, no. 81 (February 1970): 14–22.

Donovan, Robert Alan. *The Shaping Vision: Imagination in the English Novel from Defoe to Dickens.* Ithaca, N.Y.: Cornell University Press, 1966.

127

Dowling, William C. "Tristram Shandy's Phantom Audience." *Novel* 13 (1980): 284–95.

Dyson, A. E. "Sterne: The Novelist as Jester." *Critical Quarterly*, 4, no. 4 (1962): 309–20.

Engell, James, ed. *Johnson and His Age.* Cambridge and London: Harvard University Press, 1984.

Farrell, William J. "Nature Versus Art as a Comic Pattern in *Tristram Shandy.*" *ELH* 30, no. 1 (1963): 16–35.

Faurot, Ruth Marie. "Mrs. Shandy Observed." *Studies in English Literature 1500–1900* 10 (1970): 579–89.

Fluchère, Henri. *Laurence Sterne. From Tristram to Yorick: An Interpretation of* Tristram Shandy. London: Oxford University Press, 1965.

Hartley, Lodwick. " ' 'Tis a Picture of Myself': The Author in *Tristram Shandy.*" *Southern Humanities Review* 4 (1970): 301–13.

Hunter, J. Paul. "Response as Reformation: *Tristram Shandy* and the Art of Interruption." *Novel* 4 (1971): 132–46.

Karl, Frederick. *The Adversary Literature.* New York: Farrar, Straus & Giroux, 1974.

Lamb, Jonathan. "The Comic Sublime and Sterne's Fiction." *ELH* 48, no. 1 (1981): 110–43.

Macksey, Richard. " 'Alas, Poor Yorick': Sterne Thoughts." *MLN* 98 (1983): 1006–20.

Maskell, Duke. "Locke and Sterne, or Can Philosophy Influence Literature?" *Essays in Criticism* 23 (1973): 22–40.

McKee, John B. *Literary Irony and the Literary Audience: Studies in the Victimization of the Reader in Augustan Fiction.* Amsterdam: Rodopi N.V., 1974.

McMaster, Juliet. "Experience to Expression: Thematic Character Contracts in *Tristram Shandy.*" *Modern Language Quarterly* 32 (1971): 42–57.

Moglen, Helene. *The Philosophical Irony of Laurence Sterne.* Gainesville: University of Florida Press, 1975.

Myer, Valerie Grosvenor, ed. *Laurence Sterne: Riddles and Mysteries.* London and New York: Vision Press and Barnes & Noble, 1984.

Nänny, Max. "Similarity and Continuity in *Tristram Shandy.*" *English Studies* 60 (1979): 422–35.

New, Melvyn. *Laurence Sterne as Satirist: A Reading of "Tristram Shandy."* Gainesville: University of Florida Press, 1969.

Parish, Charles. "A Table of Contents for *Tristram Shandy.*" *College English* 22 (1960): 143–50.

Park, William. "*Tristram Shandy* and the New 'Novel of Sensibility.' " *Studies in the Novel* 6 (1974): 268–79.

Paulson, Ronald. *Satire and the Novel in Eighteenth-Century England.* New Haven and London: Yale University Press, 1967.

Preston, John. *The Created Self.* London: Heinemann, 1970.

Price, Martin. *To the Palace of Wisdom: Studies in Order and Energy from Dryden to Blake.* Carbondale and Edwardsville: Southern Illinois University Press, 1964.

Rosenblum, Michael. "The Sermon, the King of Bohemia, and the Art of Interpolation in *Tristram Shandy.*" *Studies in Philology* 75 (1978): 472–91.

——. "Shandean Geometry and the Challenge of Contingency." *Novel* 10 (1977): 237–47.

Shapiro, Charles, ed. *Twelve Original Essays on Great English Novels.* Detroit: Wayne State University Press, 1960.

Sherbo, Arthur. *Studies in the Eighteenth-Century English Novel.* East Lansing: Michigan State University Press, 1969.

Stedmont, John M. *The Comic Art of Laurence Sterne.* Toronto: University of Toronto Press, 1967.

Swearingen, James E. *Reflexivity in Tristram Shandy: An Essay in Phenomenological Criticism.* New Haven and London: Yale University Press, 1977.

Traugott, John, ed. *Laurence Sterne: A Collection of Critical Essays.* Englewood Cliffs, N.J.: Prentice-Hall, 1968.

———. *Tristram Shandy's World: Sterne's Philosophical Rhetoric.* Berkeley and Los Angeles: University of California Press, 1954.

Woolf, Virginia. *The Second Common Reader.* London: Hogarth Press, 1932.

Wright, Andrew. "The Artifice of Failure in *Tristram Shandy.*" *Novel* 2 (1969): 213–20.

Acknowledgments

"On *Tristram Shandy*" by Dorothy Van Ghent from *The English Novel: Form and Function* by Dorothy Van Ghent, © 1953 by Dorothy Van Ghent. Reprinted by permission of the Estate of Dorothy Van Ghent and Harper and Row Publishers.

"Art and Nature: The Duality of Man" (originally entitled "Sterne: Art and Nature II: The Duality of Man) by Martin Price from *To the Palace of Wisdom: Studies in Order and Energy from Dryden to Blake* by Martin Price, © 1964 by Martin Price. Reprinted by permission of the author.

"The Subversion of Satire" (originally entitled "Satire and Sentimentality: Sterne: The Subversion of Satire") by Ronald Paulson from *Satire and the Novel in Eighteenth-Century England* by Ronald Paulson, © 1967 by Yale University. Reprinted by permission of Yale University Press.

"The Comic Syntax of *Tristram Shandy*" by Ian Watt from *Studies in Criticism and Aesthetics, 1660–1800*, edited by Howard Anderson and John S. Shea, © 1967 by the University of Minnesota. Reprinted by permission of the University of Minnesota Press.

"Sterne: The Poetics of Sensibility" (originally entitled "Swift and Sterne: The Disturbance of Form-II Sterne: The Poetics of Sensibility") by Martin C. Battestin from *The Providence of Wit: Aspects of Form in Augustan Literature and the Arts* by Martin C. Battestin, © 1974 by Martin C. Battestin. Reprinted by permission by the University Press of Virginia and the author.

"Sterne and the Nostalgia for Reality" by Robert Alter from *Partial Magic: The Novel as a Self-Conscious Genre* by Robert Alter, © 1975 by the Regents of the University of California. Reprinted by permission of The University of California Press.

"Sterne and Swift: Augustan Continuities" by Max Byrd from *Johnson and His Age* (Harvard English Studies 12), edited by James Engell, © 1984 by the President and Fellows of Harvard College. Reprinted by permission of Harvard University Press.

Index

Ada (Nabokov), 87
Alter, Robert, 73
Auden, W. H., 116

Barthes, Roland, 90
Bate, W. Jackson, 107
Battle of the Books, The (Swift), 25, 40
Blake, William, 5, 107, 112
Bloom, Harold, 7, 107
Booth, Wayne, 79
Boswell, James, 47

Cervantes, Miguel de, 18–20, 87, 89, 92,
    93, 112
Clarissa (Richardson), 32
Coleridge, Samuel Taylor, 17–18, 19,
    112

DePorte, Michael, 110
Descartes, René, 92
Diderot, Denis, 87, 97
Don Quixote (Cervantes) as model for
    Tristram Shandy, 109: episodic struc-
    ture, 7–8; interpolated tales, 87, 89;
    juxtaposition of fantasy and reality,
    93; operations of consciousness in, 9
Dostoyevski, Fyodor, 18
Dryden, John, 63, 65, 86, 112

Epictetus, 44, 61
Erasmus, Desiderius, 37
Essay on Man (Dryden), 63, 65, 86, 112

Fielding, Henry, 1, 65, 108; narrator in,
    87, 89, 95; realism and satire in, 32;
    and Sterne compared, 23, 27, 29,
    102; villains in works of, 33. *See
    also Tom Jones*
Fowles, John, 87
Frye, Northrop, 1, 56

Garrick, David, 118
Goldsmith, Oliver, 61–62

Hobbes, Thomas, 74, 75
Hume, David, 55

Jefferson, D. W., 108
Jenny (*Tristram Shandy*), 16, 17
Johnson, Samuel, 1, 112, 113
Joseph Andrews (Fielding), 94
Journal to Eliza (Sterne), 109, 114
Journal to Stella (Swift), 109
Joyce, James, 10, 54, 100

Kafka, Franz, 18
Kant, Immanuel, 49

Le Fever (*Tristram Shandy*), death of, 49,
    52–53, 95
*Life and Opinions of Tristram Shandy,
    Gent., The. See Tristram Shandy*
Locke, John, 1, 86, 92; and ambiguity
    of language, 116; and epistemology,
    63; human isolation and, 70;

133

Locke, John, (continued)
imagination vs. reason in works of,
111, 112; judgment vs. wit in
works of, 73; and solipsism, 81;
theory of understanding offered by,
12–13, 14, 18, 54, 111

Maria (Tristram Shandy), 18–20, 75, 113,
114
Mayoux, Jean-Jacques, 97, 100, 101
Memoirs of Martin Scriblerus, The (Sterne),
26, 34–35, 37
Montaigne, Michel de, 109

Nabokov, Vladimir, 87
Newton, Sir Isaac, 92

Pascal, Blaise, 24, 27
Political Romance, A (Sterne), 38
Pope, Alexander, 2, 25, 26, 31, 37
Preston, John, 110
Price, Martin, 4, 92–93
Proust, Marcel, 1, 9–10, 54, 100

Rabelais, François, 5, 37, 114
Rawson, C. J., 121
Richardson, Jonathan, 83–84
Richardson, Samuel, 32, 94; and Sterne,
42, 96–97, 108

Sentimental Journey, A (Sterne), 83, 114
Shandy, Aunt Dinah (Tristram Shandy),
32
Shandy, Master Bobby (Tristram Shandy),
26, 56, 81, 91, 95, 101
Shandy, Mr. Toby (Tristram Shandy), 20,
71, 94, 96; and comedy of incomprehension, 26; and duality of love,
27, 28, 29; as foil to Walter, 37,
41; hobbyhorse of, 39, 65–66,
68–69, 81; as mad, 110, misinterpretation of meaning by, 62, 64,
120; providence and, 60–61; Sermon
on Conscience by, 39; Tristram's

mind and, 32; and warfare as game,
24, 25; and Widow Wadman courtship, 29, 46–47, 98, 99–100
Shandy, Tristram (Tristram Shandy): as
author, 77, 78, 79; character and
causality of, 23; as child-victim, 34,
37; conception and birth of, 13–14,
15; dialogue with reader-audience of,
33, 50–51, 52; Jenny and, 70; Maria
and, 18–20, 75, 113, 114; as mask
for Sterne, 94, 96; as metaphor,
120; mind of, 32, 33, 37; as
"modern" man, 60, 63; Nanette
and, 4, 72–73; as narrator, 59;
parents of, 43–44; as performer, 90;
present moment and, 33; providence
and, 60–61; roles of, 34, 37, 51, 59,
60, 63, 90; sentimental journey of,
4; sexualizing of language by, 117;
story of, 76; and Teller (Tale of a
Tub), 59–60; and writing as conversation, 82
Shandy, Mr. Walter (Tristram Shandy):
feelings and, 24; hypothesis and, 38,
66, 67, 68, 70; and imagination vs.
reality, 36; as mad, 110; names and,
23; theories of, and their consequences, 23, 34, 35; theories of, in
Tristram's mind, 32, 36, 37; on
time, 14, 62; verbal intercourse and,
64; as villain, 34, 35, 36, 38; words
and, 25–26, 29
Shandy, Mrs. Walter (Tristram Shandy):
association of ideas and, 54–55; conception of hero by, 13–14; conversation and conception of hero, 44–45
Shandy, Uncle Toby. See Shandy, Mr.
Toby
Shandys, The (Tristram Shandy), and
mind vs. imagination, 60; sensuality
of, 71, 72–73; and sexual matters,
69, 70, 72; universe of, 61; world
of, 62
Slawenbergius's tale, 28, 70, 89–90, 104
Slop, Dr. (Tristram Shandy), 20, 31, 39,
40, 98, 108
Smollett, Tobias George, 31, 38, 96
Spitzer, Leo, 59

Sterne, Laurence: ambiguity of language and, 82–83; and association as method, 101, 102–4; Augustans and, 1, 2, 77, 108–21; cervantic humor of, 20–21, 112; communication forms, used by, 40, 42, 83–84; and creative process in novel, 10–11; and doctrine of Sensibility, 1, 4, 12–13, 18; and duality of love, 2–4, 28, 74; and duality of man, 27–28, 75, 93; eccentricity of, 96, 107, 111; fantasy and, 97, 101; Fielding and, 23, 29; and humor and sentiment coexistence, 52–54, 55; images in, 108, 119, 120; imagination of, 13, 64–65, 73–74, 75, 81, 82, 83, 112–13; influence of Locke on, 12–13, 18; judgment and separation in, 73; literary conventions and, 42, 89, 107; and madness as metaphor, 111, 114; mimesis and, 86; mind and, 63–64, 66, 104, 113; models for, 96; predecessors and, 108; Rabelais and, 114; realism of, 93, 97–98, 100, 101; reason vs. imagination in, 64–65, 71, 75; Richardson and, 96–97; and sensibility and experience, 85; sensual and, 4–5; sexual wit of, 95; solipsism vs. imagination, 81, 82, 83; sources of his work, 109; studies of, 43; syntax of, 48; theory of knowledge, 29, 71, 85; timelessness and technique of, 79, 80–81; Tristram Shandy and, 94; understanding and, 42, 82; unifying relations and imagination of, 73–74; and words and forms, 29, 39–40, 82
Stevens, Wallace, 1
Suard, M., 12
Swift, Jonathan: influence on Sterne of, 31, 108, 109; madness as theme, 111, and metaphor and truth, 118–19; and reality and fantasy; 121, and reality and order, 40; and reason and sense, 60; satiric allegory of, 116, 117, 118; scatology and sexual humor of, 114–15, 116; Sterne's subversion of, 42; and truth and interpretation, 117, 118. See also Tale of a Tub, A; Journal to Stella

Tale of a Tub, A (Swift), 29, 31, 32, 33; chaos in, 37, 75; intellectual impotence of, 38–39; madness theme in, 75, 110, 111; misinterpretation in, 118; order in, 40, 66; as parody of Sterne, 121; satiric allegory in, 116, 117, 118; sublimation in, 114–15; Teller and, 59–60; Tristram Shandy and, 109
Tale of Two Lovers, 88–89, 90–91, 97, 98
Tave, Stuart, 31
Toby, Uncle. See Shandy, Mr. Toby
Tom Jones (Fielding): Augustan ethos in, 63; balance of mind in, 27; as drama 8, 18; irrational vs. verbal communication in, 42; narrators in, 94; as parable and paradigm, 61–62; time and, 79
Traugott, John, 55, 110
Trim, Corporal: and Beguine episode, 28, 97–98; and his brother Tom, 26–27, 91, 98; comedy of incomprehension and, 26–27; and courtship of Bridget, 98; and death of Toby and mortality, 56, 101; Widow Wadman and, 98, 99–100
Tristram Shandy, 8; apostrophe in, 103; association in, 12–13, 32, 101; associative method of, 92; Augustan aesthetics in, 27, 47, 59, 76, 77; Augustan tradition and, 72–73, 74, 75, 113; the bawdy in, 75, 82–83, 114, 116, 117; and body language, sensuality of, 84–85; characterization in, 23, 29; Coleridge's definition of humor and, 17–18, 20; as comedy of self-contained mind, 25–26, 29; comic syntax in, 43–57; communication in, 39, 40–42; conception of hero in, 44–46; concreteness of visualization in, 13, 15, 16; consciousness in, 9–10, 11–12, 15, 16; conversation in, 45–48, 50, 57; creative process

Tristram Shandy, *(continued)*
in, 10–11; death and mortality in,
17, 80; death in, 95–96; and death
of Bobby, 26, 56, 81, 91, 95, 101;
and death of Le Fever, 49, 52–53,
95; and death of Tristram, 80; and
death of Yorick, 79, 81, 95; fantasy
in, 103, 104; hobbyhorse metaphor
in, 53, 65–66, 67–68, 69, 81;
imagination vs. reason in, 64–65, 84;
imitation in, 75, 76, 78, 86; impotence theme in, 24, 38, 39, 101,
103; incongruity and humor in, 17,
20–21, 28; interpolation of tales in,
18–20, 75, 87, 88–89, 113, 114;
isolation and separation in, 37,
81–82; literary convention in, 94;
madness of characters in, 110,
113–14; Maria-Tristram tale in,
18–20, 75, 113, 114; and mimesis,
77, 86; misinterpretation in, 62, 64,
120; movement in, 104; narrative
voice vs. narrative event in, 43–45;
narrator in, 93, 94; onomatopoetic
devices in, 85; and parody in Lovers,
88–89, 90–91, 93, 97, 98, 110;
Quixote-Sancho pairings in, 93;
reality in, 39, 75, 88, 101; satire in,
31, 33, 34, 37, 38; as self-conscious
novel, 87, 88; as self-reflexive fiction, 105–6; sensation and association, 12–13, 77, 120; Sermon on
Conscience, 39–40; *Tale of a Tub* influence on, 109–10; time in, 14–16,
17, 79, 80–81; typography of, 48,
50, 77, 88, 89, 90, 91, 95, 99, 100,
103; and unity of the comic, 43, 47,
54, 57, 75, 119, 120; view of man
in, 60, 63; visual devices in, 84;
words in, 29, 39, 40–41; world of,
91–92
Tuveson, Ernest, 55

Wadman, Mrs. Widow, 4, 46, 47, 48,
94, 98–99, 100
Wasserman, Earl, 59, 75
Watkins, W. B. C., 4

Yeats, William Butler, 57
Yorick, Mr.: death of, 79, 81, 95; and
Maria, 113, 114; as priest, 24; as
satanic villain, 38; as satirist/isolate,
37; in Shakespeare, 54; in Tristram's
mind, 32, 40